Painting with Gouache

MICHAEL SANDERS

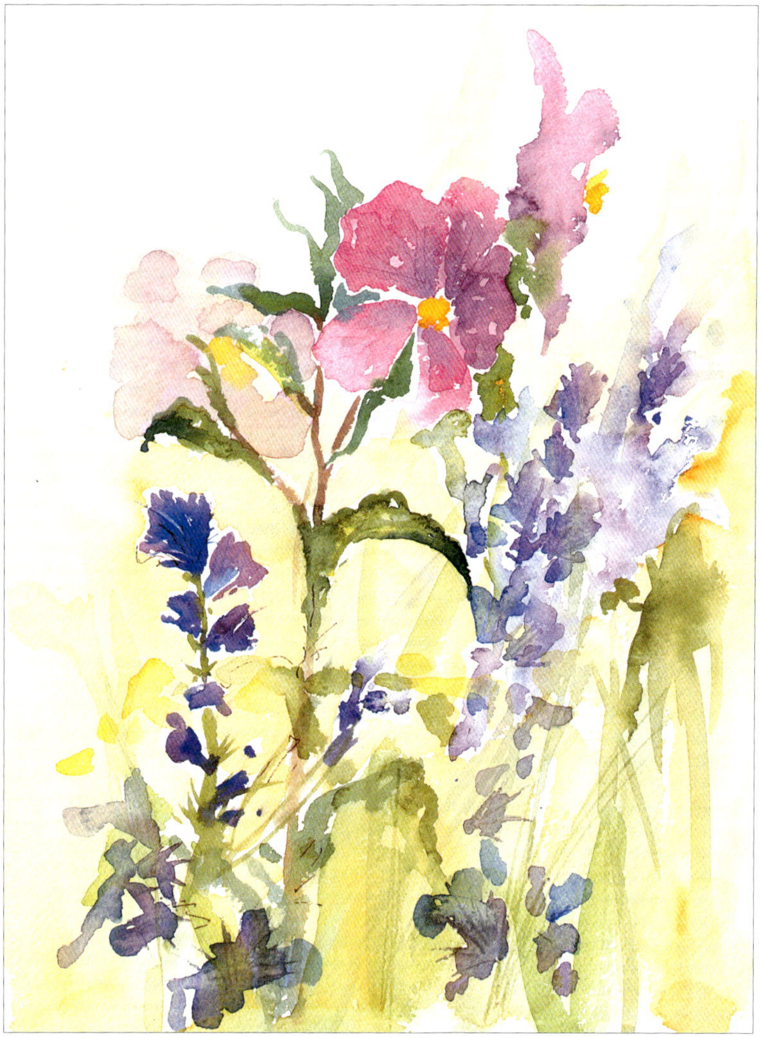

SEARCH PRESS

First published in Great Britain 2005

Search Press Limited
Wellwood, North Farm Road,
Tunbridge Wells, Kent TN2 3DR

Photographs by Charlotte de la Bédoyère, Search Press Studios

ISBN 1 84448 046 1

The Publishers and author can accept no responsibility for any consequences arising from the information, advice or instructions given in this publication.

The Publishers would like to thank Winsor & Newton for supplying some of the materials used in this book.

Suppliers

If you have difficulty in obtaining any of the materials or equipment mentioned in this book, then please visit the Search Press website for details of suppliers: www.searchpress.com

Alternatively, you can write to the Publishers at the address above, for a current list of stockists, including firms that operate a mail-order service, or you can write to Winsor & Newton requesting a list of distributors.

Winsor & Newton, UK Marketing
Whitefriars Avenue, Harrow,
Middlesex, HA3 5RH

Publisher's note

All the step-by-step photographs in this book feature the author, Michael Sanders, demonstrating his gouache painting techniques. No models have been used.

There are references to animal hair brushes in this book. It is the Publishers' custom to recommend synthetic materials as substitutes for animal products wherever possible. There is now a large range of brushes available made from artificial fibres, and they are satisfactory substitutes for those made from natural fibres.

Manufactured by Classicscan Pte Ltd, Singapore

Printed in Malaysia by Times Offset (M) Sdn Bhd

To all my watercolour students, who have asked so many questions about gouache that I felt this book was almost inevitable! Thanks to anyone who ever said, 'I've got a tube or two of that, but don't know what to do with it'. I hope the answers will be found within.

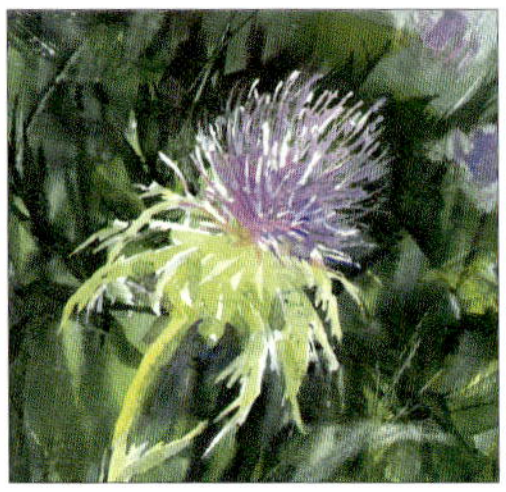

I would like to thank all at Search Press, especially Sophie, who put up with my erratic computer, and Lotti, Juan and Roz, for making the whole process so enjoyable.

Cover

Painting in Andalucia

280 x 360mm (11 x 14¼in)

This is an example of gouache used very thinly, like watercolour. The cork oak tree foliage was applied with a sponge, using very dilute paint, allowing the light and dark sides to blend. I am particularly pleased with the little group of picnickers under the tree. They were painted right at the end, using opaque paint. The whole image has a light, airy look, but with strong directional light.

Page 1

Wild Flowers

255 x 330mm (10 x 13in)

This little group of wild flowers was painted on one of my painting holidays as a demonstration. I am pleased with the pale, warm, creamy background and the delicate balance between transparent and opaque paint. It is subtle without being wishy-washy.

Opposite

Spanish Cork Oaks

170 x 195mm (6¾ x 7¾in)

This is another demonstration, painted for a group on one of my holidays. The area was very remote. We were about to set up a picnic, when I noticed this little lane running down to a derelict farm, and I particularly liked the way the light came through the trees. When it was nearly finished, I wanted to imply the purple flowers on the right-hand side, rather than paint them in detail, so I simply splashed some paint on. The idea being that, if it didn't work, I could use an opaque method and hide the mistake. As it happened, it worked well, so the picnic was not delayed!

Contents

Introduction 4

Materials 6

Colour 12

Tone 14

Three elements of a painting 16

Composition 18

Techniques 20

Landscape 22
Step-by-step

Flowers 32
Step-by-step

Mediterranean River 40
Step-by-step

Index 48

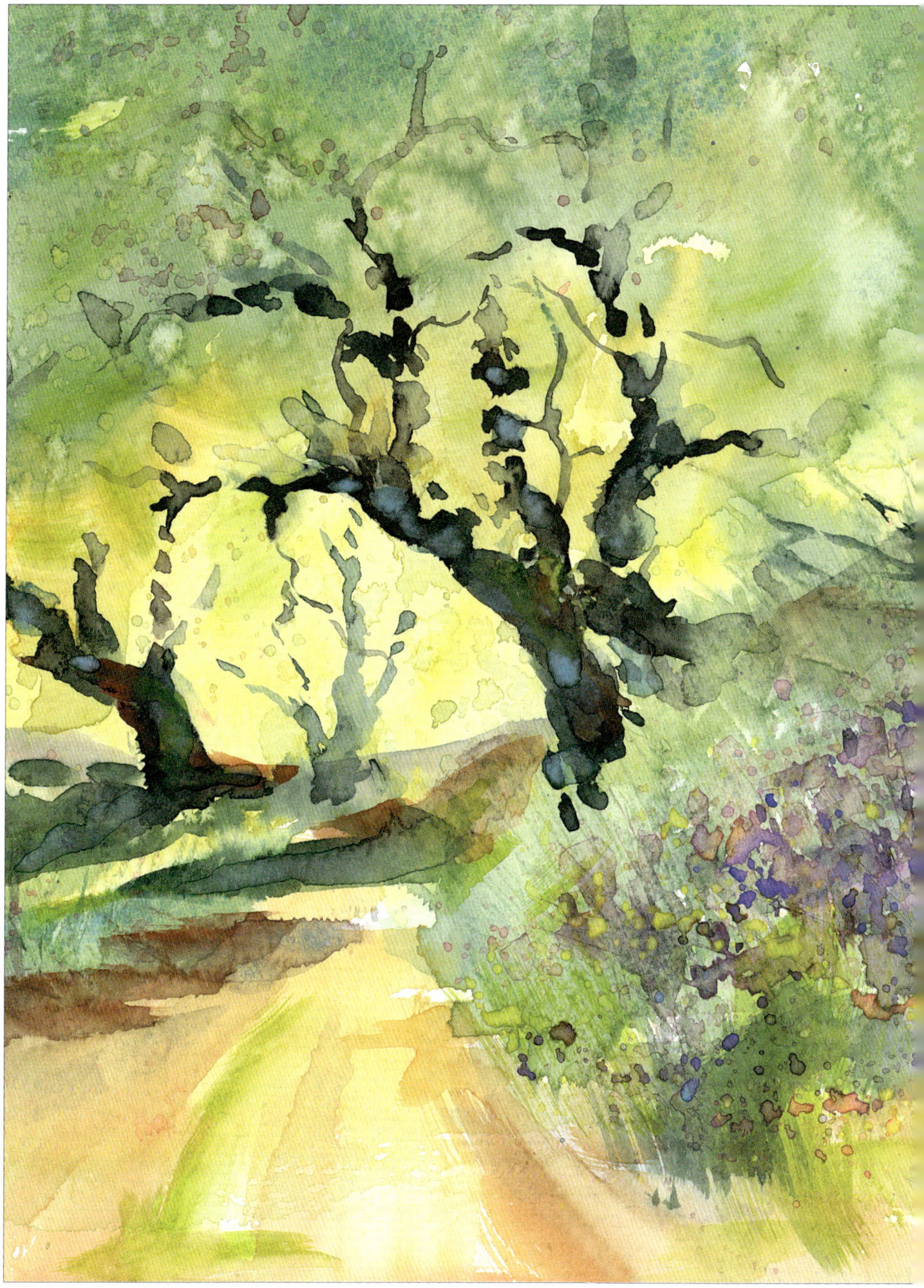

Introduction

I have always enjoyed using gouache, right from the time I first encountered the medium when I was at art college in the 1960s and training to be a graphic artist.

At the time I used it purely as a design material, utilising especially the quick-drying opacity, and its ability to cover an area with flat colour.

Several years later I was drawn to experiment with gouache as a painting medium suitable for fine art, when painting for pleasure. I have been using it ever since, and I particularly like the flexibility it offers; opaque when diluted only slightly with water, transparent when diluted further.

The variety of surfaces available to paint on increases dramatically when using gouache, especially when compared with watercolour: I prefer working directly on to coloured card, allowing the background colour to show through here and there as a unifying influence.

Many of the images in this book were painted out of doors, on site, and this is where the paint really comes into its own. There is the flexibility of using an opaque medium, the speed of drying, the textural effects possible when using a sponge, or similar, to paint with, and the combination of subtlety and vibrancy – all in one paint.

So, you might ask, who is this book suitable for? Perhaps you are starting in art for the first time and want a simple, fun medium that is easy to learn and uncomplicated to use. Maybe you have used watercolours, and would like to add an extra dimension to your technique. You might be an oil painter who would like an opaque paint that is quick drying and easy to transport, with no need for solvents or oils.

Whatever your experience or background in art, this book is for you. Welcome to the world of gouache painting.

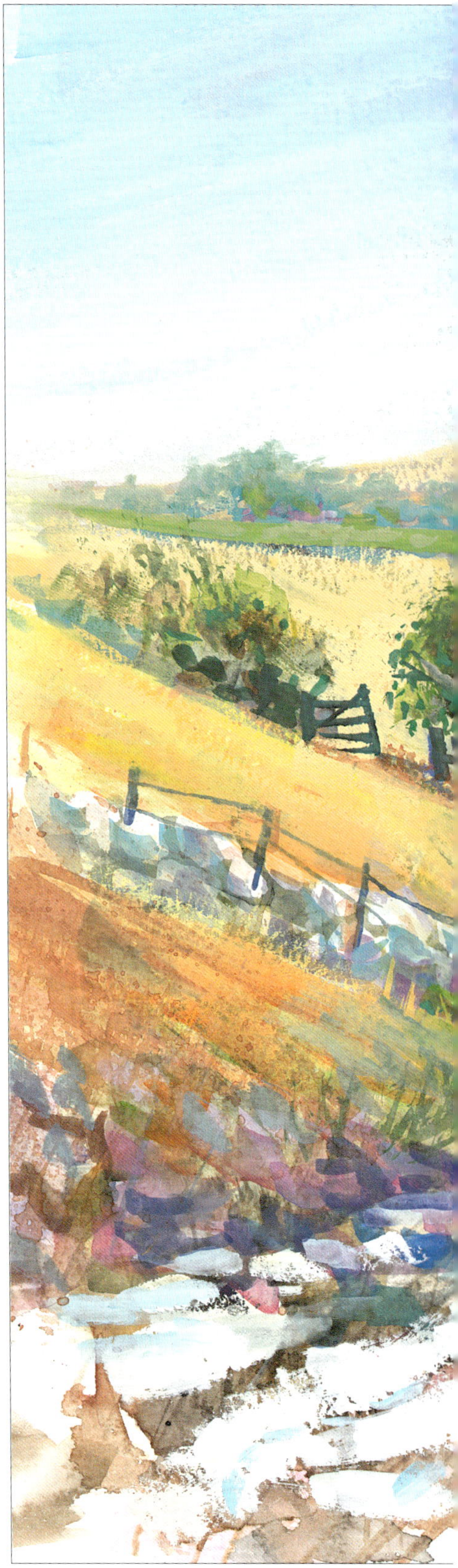

Tavy Cleave, Dartmoor

340 x 265mm (13½ x 10½in)

Making a painting like this would have been difficult in any other medium. This was a fairly remote, windy spot, so carrying a large selection of heavy oil painting equipment out there would have been very hard. If I had tried to paint this scene in watercolour, the paper could easily have blown over, staining or damaging it and ruining the painting. With a small, well-chosen selection of gouache colours and a piece of tinted card, I was able to paint this evocative scene using just two brushes and a bit of sponge. This is one reason why I love gouache!

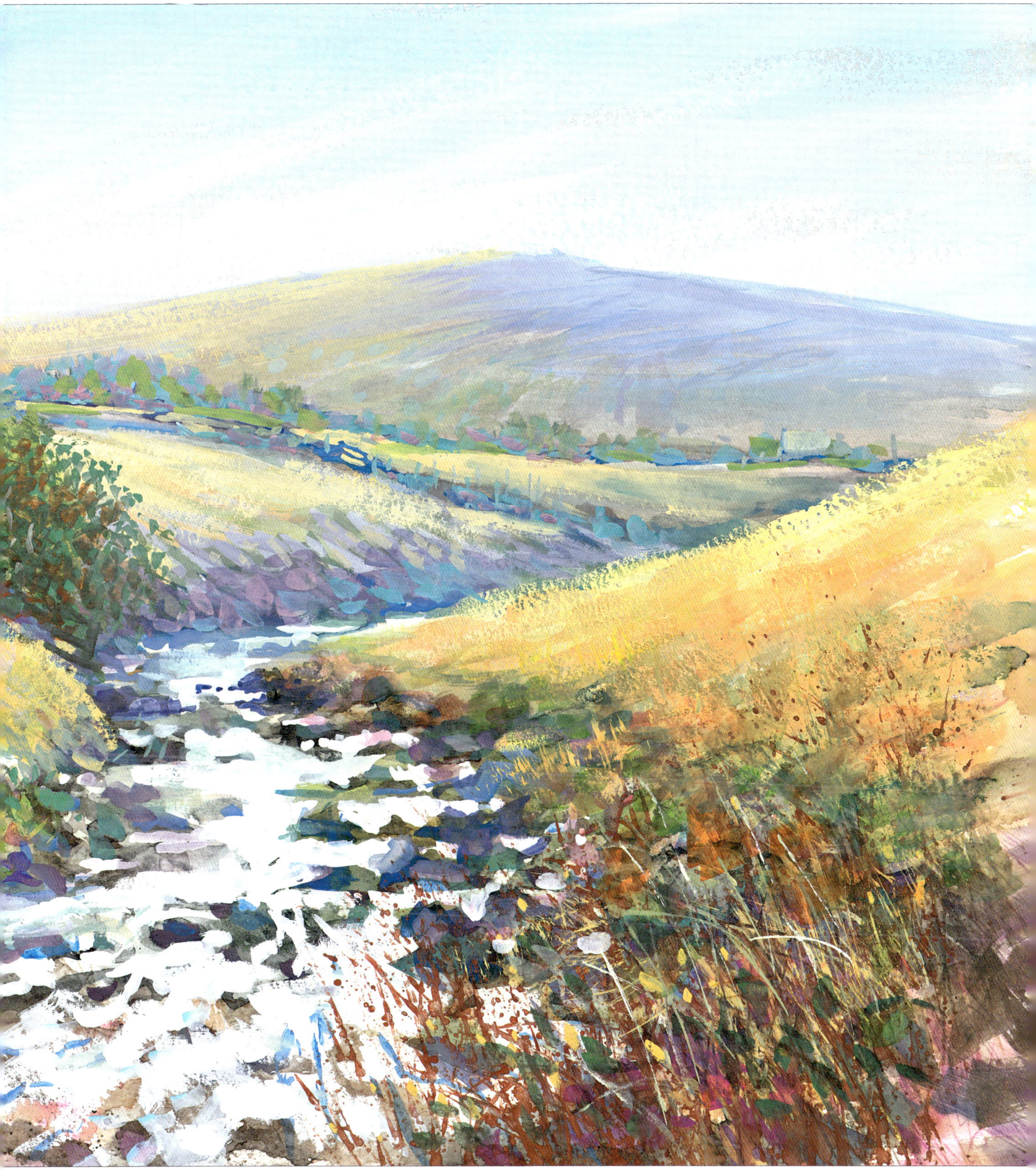

Materials

Paints

Also known as 'body colour', gouache is an opaque version of watercolour that uses the same kind of pigments as the transparent kind. The binding agent that holds the paint together is usually gum arabic. The paint film is thicker than watercolour, and the paint often contains glycerine for flexibility, making it more soluble in water. For this reason, you do not need quite as much water as for watercolours. How much you need is something you can learn only through trial and error.

The most important property of the material is its opacity. To achieve this, higher levels of pigment are used than for watercolours, at least in the better quality ranges. The opacity is often increased by the addition of barium sulphate or, in the cheaper kinds, a chemically treated chalk. In the cheapest paints of all, coloured chalk is used extensively to give them the opacity. Always buy the best you can afford – if the words 'artist's quality' or 'designer's quality' appear on the label, that is a good sign.

Although the paint is opaque when moderately diluted, if thinned with additional amounts of water it will become almost as transparent as traditional watercolour, especially the best quality gouache. Generally, when thinned in this way, they are almost, but not quite, as brilliant as they are when less diluted. Some of the more transparent pigments, such as burnt sienna, work very well applied as a weaker wash: other more opaque colours, such as the cadmiums, need to be used fairly thick.

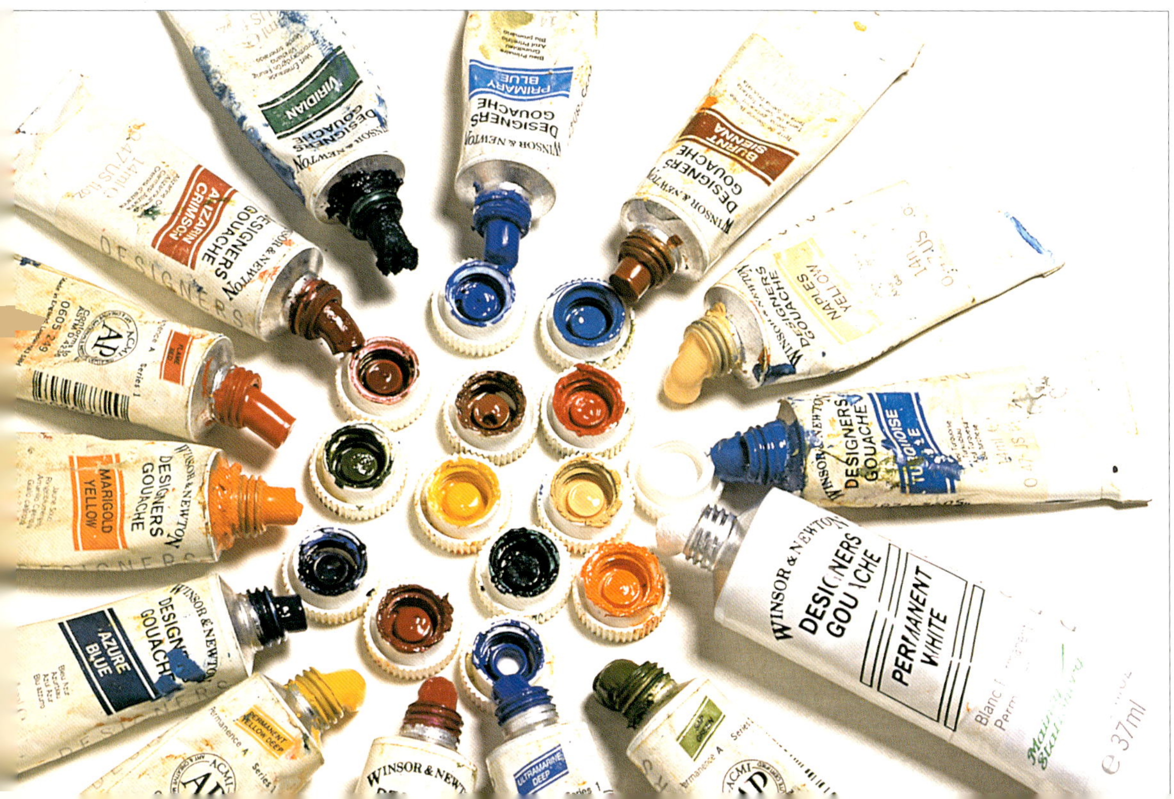

Choosing colours

There is a huge range of colours on the market and making a choice can appear quite daunting, especially to the beginner. Don't worry – you will not need them all!

If you are just starting out, I recommend keeping your colours to a minimum, until you get the hang of mixing those, then you can add some of the others, depending on the subjects you find interesting to paint. I have a palette of about fifteen colours, but rarely use all of them in one painting.

I have a very simple selection process when choosing my colours – whatever medium I happen to be using – based on the three primaries: yellow, red and blue. To use this method successfully you need to understand a little about colour temperature. This entails deciding whether a colour is 'warm' or 'cold'. An acidic lemon yellow looks entirely different to a rich, deep, marigold yellow. The one that appears to have a touch of red in it – marigold yellow – is the warm one: lemon yellow is cold. With reds, a bright orangey red is warm, whereas magenta, a deep purple red that looks as if it has a touch of blue in, must be cold. A warm blue such as ultramarine will tend towards violet, compared with a cold blue like Prussian. This becomes more apparent if a touch of white is added to each. That gives us six colours – a warm and a cold version of yellow, red and blue.

A white is essential to mix light colours, especially when painting on coloured card. I also like to have a sap green, a burnt sienna and a Naples yellow. From this range it is possible to make a huge variety of other colours; it would make a good starting set to add to as you go along.

I have made additions to this simple set: my complete palette is lemon yellow, marigold yellow, permanent yellow deep, Naples yellow, flame red, alizarin crimson, magenta, ultramarine blue, primary blue, azure blue, Prussian blue, turquoise, sap green burnt sienna and permanent white.

This is my personal choice, so you may well end up with a different range, depending on the subject you have selected. I have several blues, for instance, because I spend quite a lot of time running painting holidays in Mediterranean areas, and feel I need them to cope with different sea colours. I don't use black; I find a mix of ultramarine and burnt sienna makes a lovely, interesting dark colour.

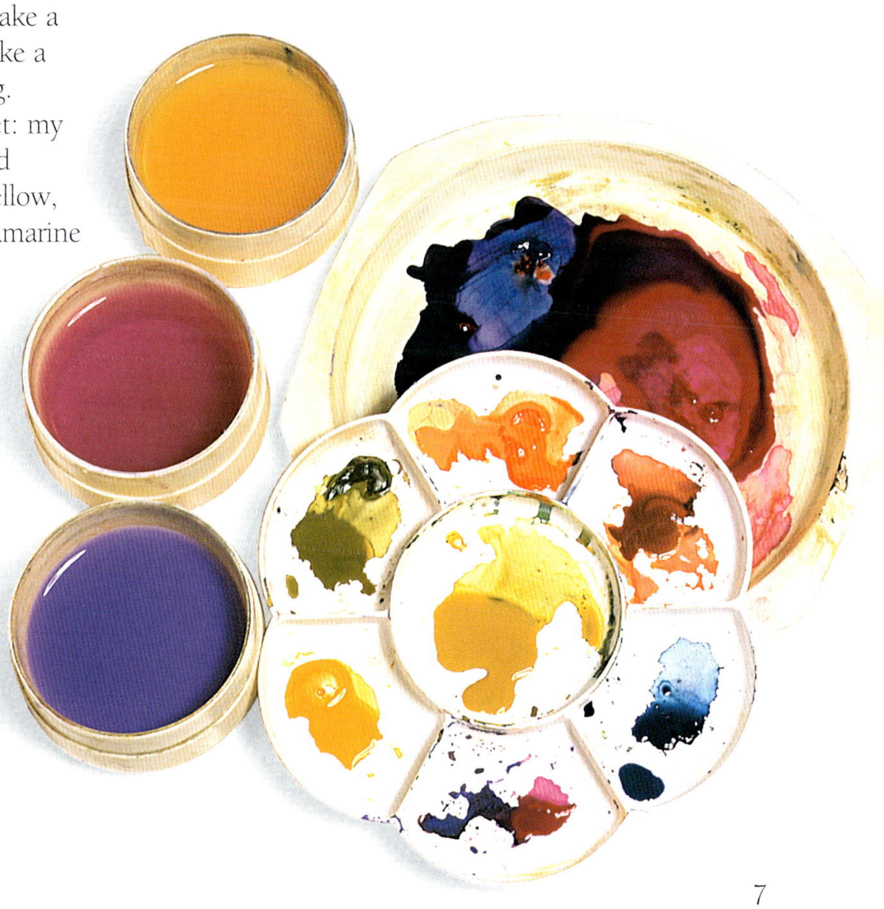

Surfaces

With gouache it is possible to paint on coloured paper and card, as well as the whole range of watercolour papers. This can be done because you do not have to use the white of the paper, as you would in watercolour, to lighten a colour or provide a white area. When using the opaque gouache technique, white paint is used to make colours lighter, or to add white areas. There are many creative techniques available that allow the colour of the surface to play a part in our work. I like working on a brown, cream or a blue/grey card, and sometimes a burgundy red or maroon. Almost any absorbent, non-shiny surface will take gouache, as long as it is not greasy or oily or has a wax surface. Some makes of gouache have poor adhesion on shiny surfaces.

The choice of background colour will depend on several factors: personal preference, the nature of the subject and the mood or atmosphere you want to evoke all play a part.

If you cannot find exactly the right colour card or paper to fit your requirements, it is possible to take some watercolour paper and tint it with a light wash of acrylic paint, thinned with a lot of water, so that when dry, the paper retains its absorbency.

A selection of surfaces showing how gouache is affected by different background colours.

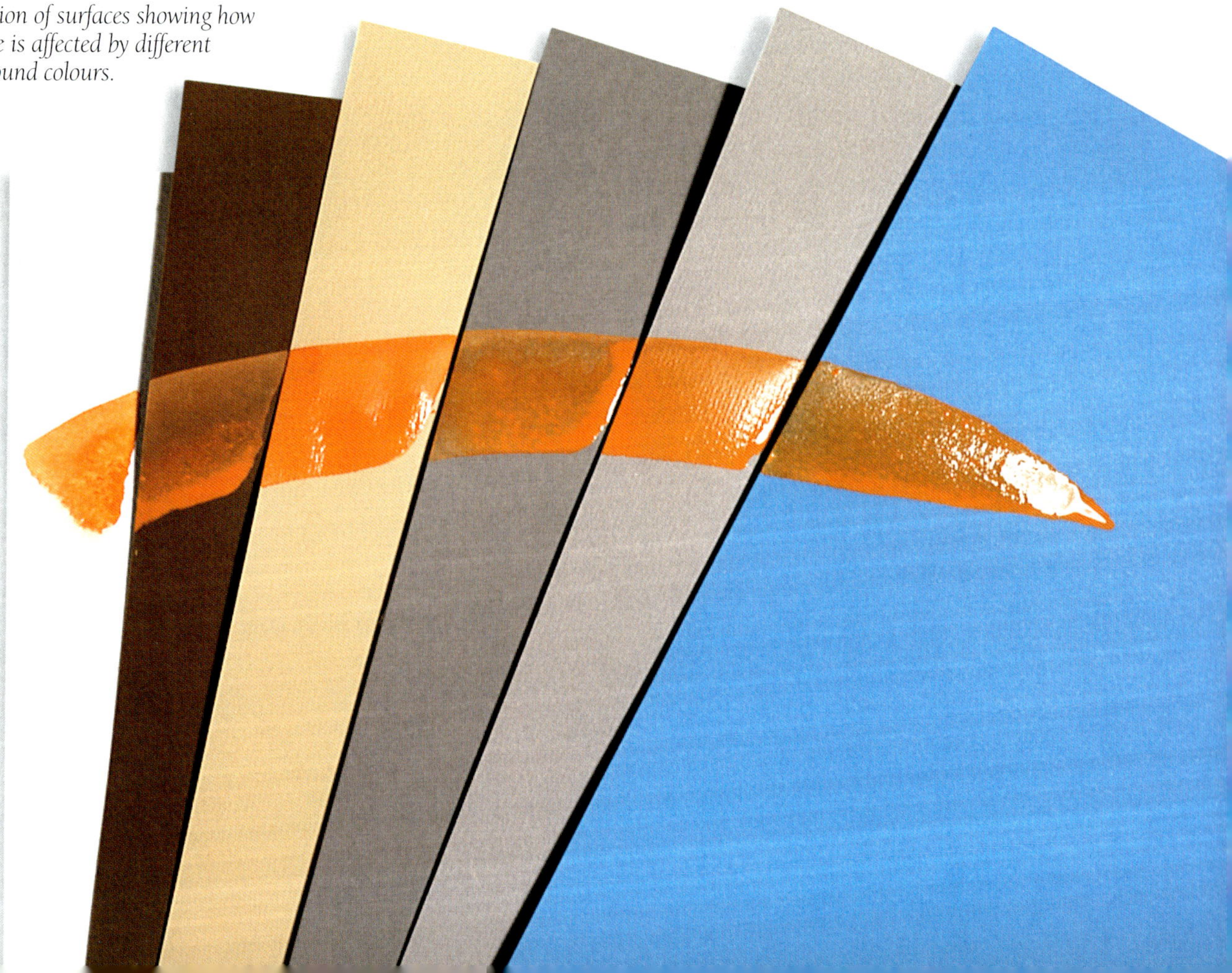

How backgrounds affect colours

Gouache paint really comes into its own when used on coloured card or paper. The opacity of the paint can be used to great effect, and, if diluted, this background can show through each colour to modify it. Here are my fifteen colours, painted in different dilutions on white, and also on a warm and a cool surface. White has been added to the right-hand side of each colour to make it paler; this is called a 'tint'.

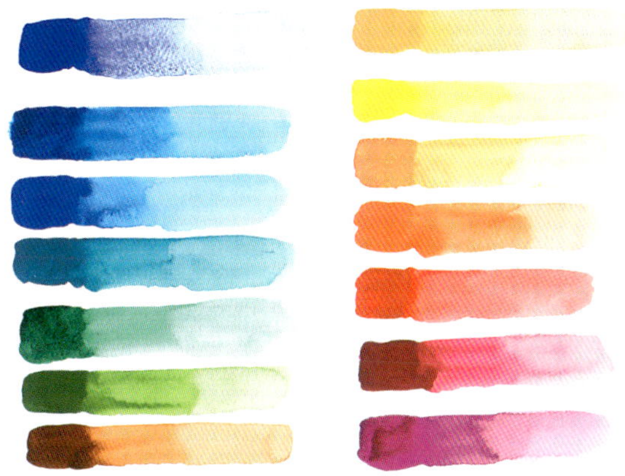

These colours have been applied on rough watercolour paper. The left-hand side of each colour strip is slightly diluted with water, the next more diluted, and the right-hand side is slightly diluted with white added. Heavyweight paper works best.

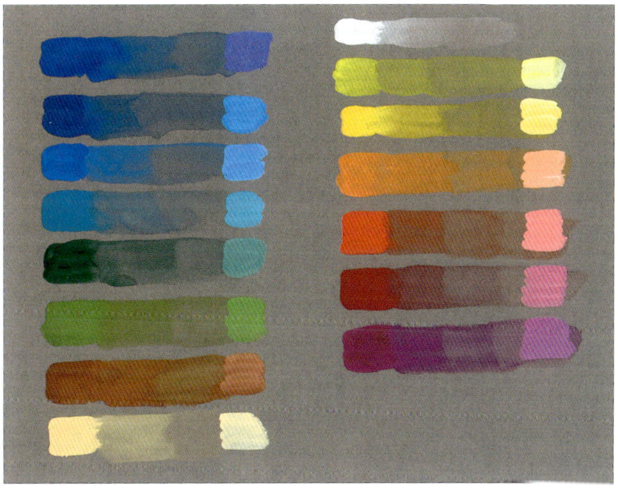

On this cooler surface, the thinner applications look different. Blues look slightly grey and yellows have a green tinge to them, while the reds have turned slightly brown. When lightened with white, the colours do not look as intense as they do on the brown card, because the brown is darker and offers more contrast. All of these properties can be used in our paintings.

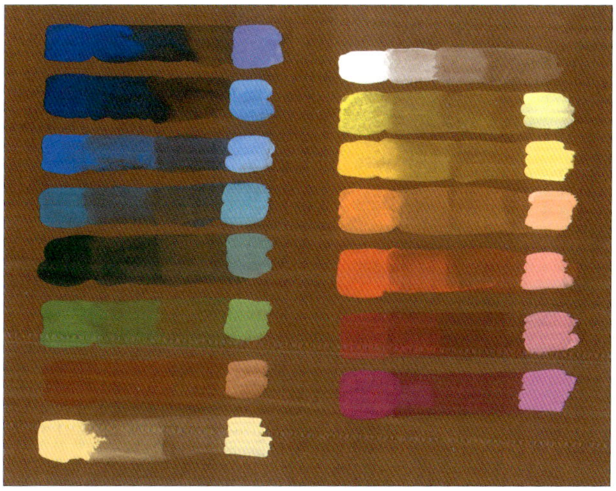

Here is the same range of colours applied in the same way as opposite, this time on brown card. You can clearly see how the colour of the card shows through where they are diluted most, adding a warm tinge to each. See also how the white paint, added to each colour on the right-hand side, strengthens and intensifies it, making it more striking.

Using gouache in this way, where the colour of the surface is part of the painting process, is very important, and I advise you to get some card or paper of varying colours, and make some strips like this, keeping notes beside each one to remind you of the characteristics of each, and how the background colour affects them.

Brushes

If you are a watercolourist, you will probably already have a few favourite brushes; these will also be suitable for use with gouache. If you are new to art or do not have much equipment, here are a few guidelines for buying some. Avoid the very cheap brushes that come in a pack – as with anything else, you get what you pay for. Your brushes are the point of contact between you and the painting so should be purchased with care. Buy a few good quality ones, clean them after each use and store them carefully.

I like to use an oriental brush called a hake to apply even layers of paint quickly and easily. These are relatively cheap and very versatile. I have a 2.5cm (1in) one and a 5cm (2in) one. The best type to get are the ones where the hair is stitched into a split wooden handle, that is without any metal part.

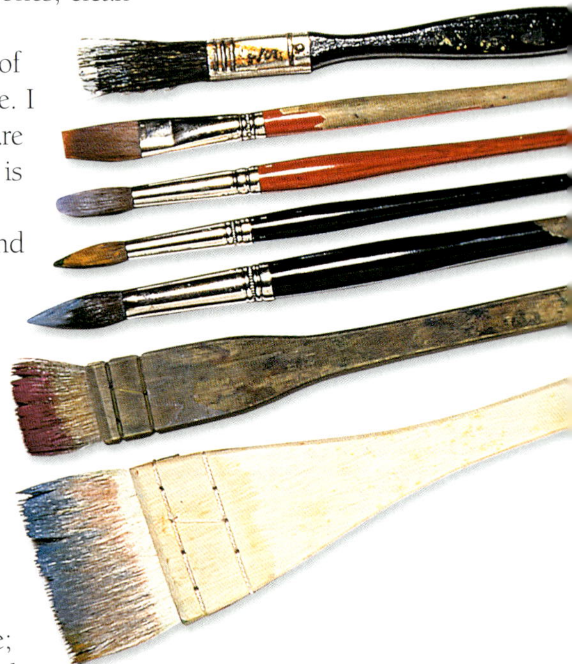

Watercolour brushes come in a huge range of types and sizes, and are usually described by a number, with the higher numbers denoting larger brushes. For years, the best ones were considered to be sable, but the modern synthetic hair is now every bit as good, much cheaper, and lasts just as long if not longer. A good brush should last you for many years and will become like a trusted friend, reliable and familiar, so look after it!

I suggest a large (no. 10 or 12) round synthetic sable, a smaller one (no. 6 or 8), and a small (no. 2), plus a 1.25cm (½in) flat brush, sometimes called a single stroke brush. Complete your set with a small household paintbrush for spattering and generally splashing about with. Buy a new one and restrict its use to gouache; you do not want to risk contaminating a painting with household oil paint by mistake.

Easels

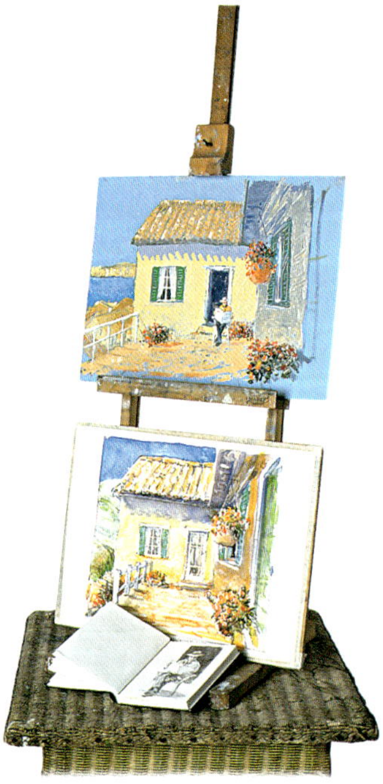

It is easier to paint with the surface at a slight angle, so a board with a block of wood or something similar wedged under the top to raise it will do. If you feel more comfortable with the work at a steeper angle, you may want to consider buying an easel. There are many types available, from the simple wooden table easel to the portable outdoor type or the complex, studio kind. Working out of doors is a very satisfying experience, but if you feel that you are never going to want to, a small table easel will be sufficient. You can get one complete with an attached box to keep your paints in if you wish.

If you are planning to venture into the great outdoors to paint, a lightweight sketching easel will not only hold the work steady but will also make you look the part! The main thing is to ensure you are comfortable as you work. Strains and aches and pains won't help your enjoyment of painting, and that is the top priority; you should enjoy it. So make sure you do not stoop, stretch or sit awkwardly.

Other equipment

A very important piece of equipment to have is a board, slightly larger than the size of painting you feel comfortable with. I have several of varying sizes, made from plywood or MDF. I like to have a rope connected to each one to serve as a carrying handle. You can fix your painting to this board using bulldog clips or masking tape. In addition to this I have a pair of scissors, some small sketchbooks and pencils and a roll or two of absorbent kitchen paper. A painting knife is useful for scraping off paint, such as in the sgraffito technique.

To complete the 'tool kit' I recommend a couple of natural sponges, an oil painter's palette knife, masking fluid, several plastic palettes with deep wells and a few jam jars for water. If you want to try spattering or lifting out, you will need some thin card for making masks or templates.

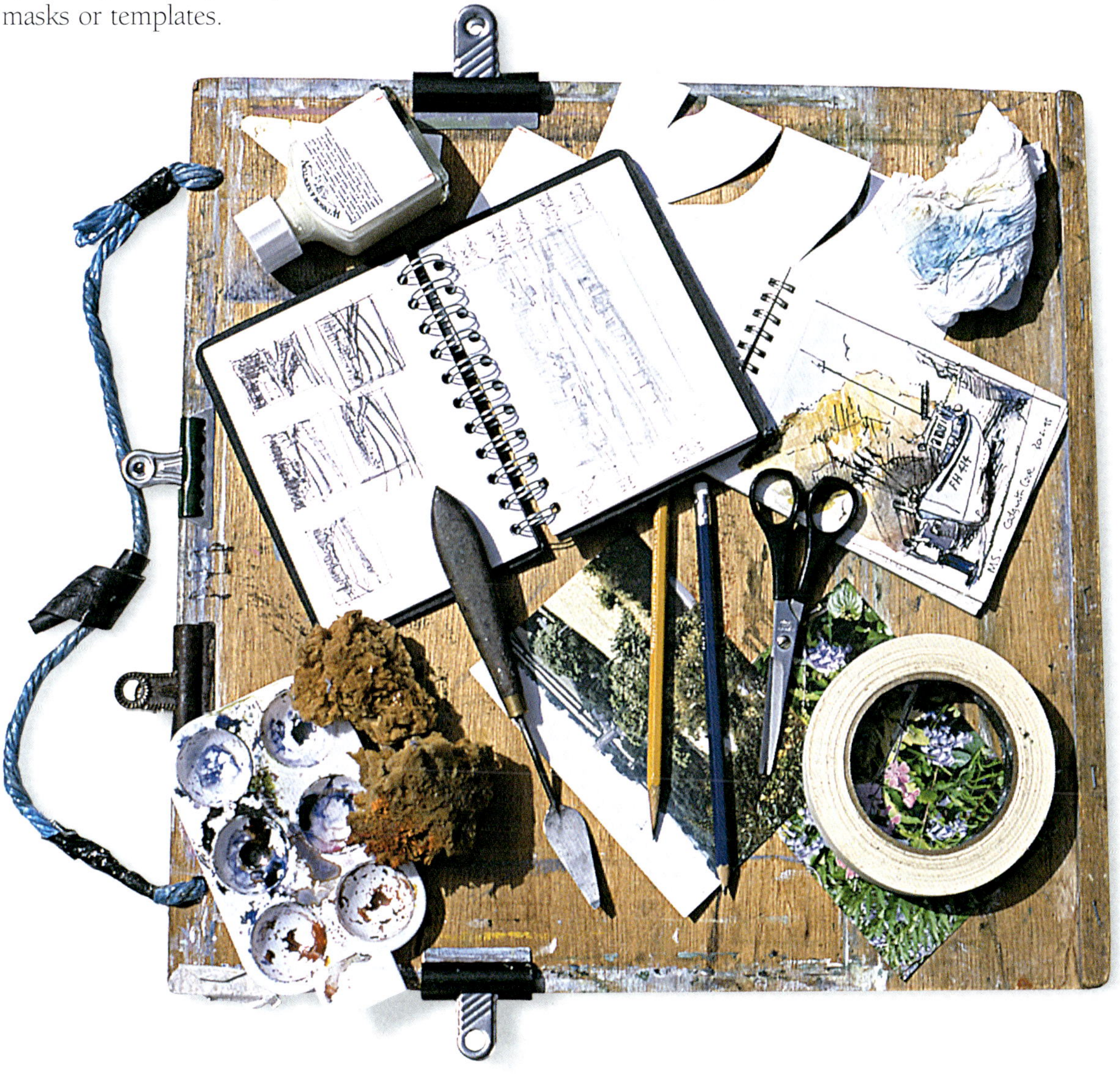

Colour

Choice of colour in a painting is a very personal thing. To start with, the main thing to learn is how to mix colours to get a larger range, and how they interact with each other. It is very useful to make a colour wheel like the one here, so that you can see how colours mix, and to get some practice in painting with gouache. You will need some white watercolour paper, lemon yellow, marigold yellow, flame red, magenta, ultramarine and primary blue, a palette, a brush, and a couple of jars of water, one to wash your brush and the other to dip into for mixing. It is important to keep your water clean; change it regularly.

Start by drawing round a small plate with a pencil on the paper. Then apply some lemon yellow inside the circle at about the eight o'clock position.

The paint should be thinned slightly with water, but not too much, until it resembles double cream in consistency. To this colour on the palette, add a touch of marigold yellow. Working clockwise, paint a thin strip of this darker, warmer yellow next to the lemon. Add a little more and paint another strip. After three strips you should be applying marigold yellow alone.

Next, add a tiny amount of flame red. Paint more strips in the same way, adding red as you go. This will make a nice orange and orange red. Flame red, on its own, should be just before the twelve o'clock position. Continue, adding little touches of magenta to the red to darken it. You will notice it is now also looking cooler when compared to the bright red you started with. Magenta should be somewhere near two o'clock.

Before moving to the blue-green section of the wheel, clean your brush to avoid muddying your colours. Add a tiny amount of ultramarine to the magenta and you'll see a violet red. Continue adding more touches of blue in the next few strips and you'll get a nice deep violet, then blue violet. You may need to add a tiny touch of white to these darker colours. Violet should be opposite the yellow on the wheel. After the ultramarine section, paint a strip consisting of ultramarine and primary blue mixed together. This should be opposite to the orange section.

When you have arrived at the primary blue colour (at about five o'clock), add a tiny touch of lemon yellow to create a turquoise blue-green. More yellow in adjacent strips will give you mid-green, yellow-green and finally, next to the lemon we started with, a nice clean lime. The greens should be opposite the reds.

If you like, you can take a clean, wet brush and, starting with the lemon and working clockwise, draw some of the paint from the strips into the centre to thin it, and make a paler tint of each colour.

Note

As you paint, don't forget to add tiny amounts of water; if you have been used to watercolour, you will have to resist the temptation to add too much!

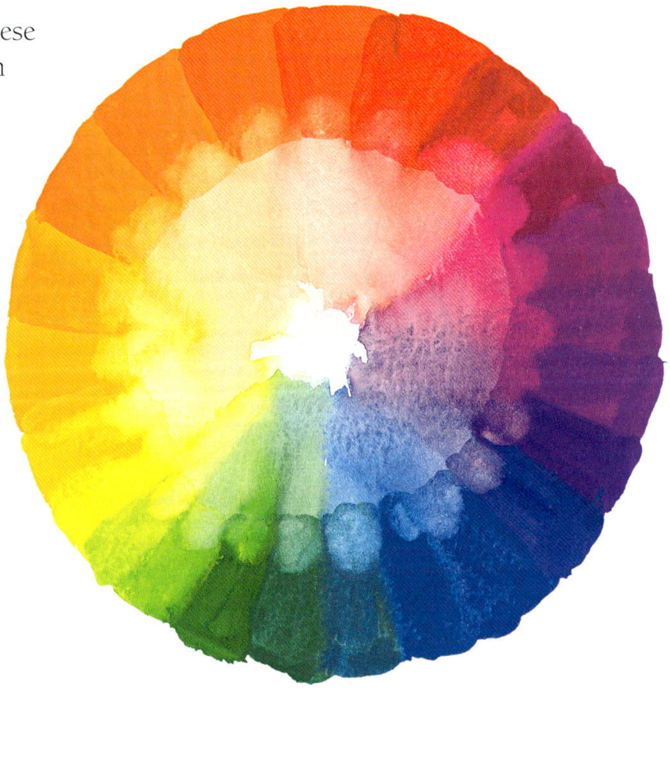

Complementary colours

If you have painted your wheel accurately, you will have a visual guide to one of the most important concepts of using colour, the complementary colour theory. This method of using colour has been used for centuries, and received particular attention in the later nineteenth century at the height of the Impressionist era. Put simply, it means that colours that are opposite one another on the wheel will look good together. They will make a 'complementary' colour scheme.

A painting that is predominantly green will look good with some touches of red, and likewise for blue with orange, and violet with yellow. Also, in order to 'tone down' or modify a colour to make it less bright, a complementary can be mixed in with it.

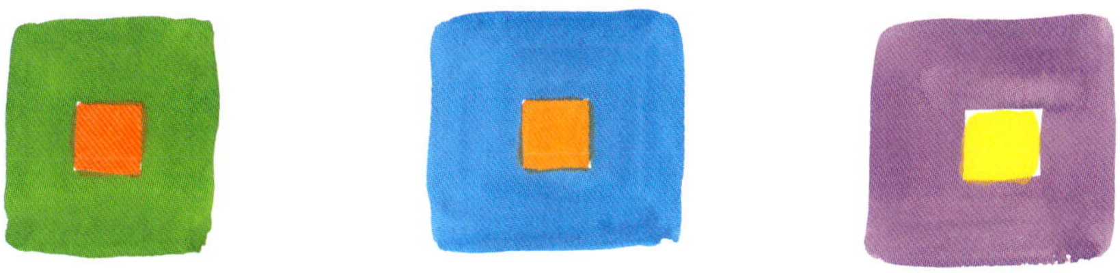

Large colour squares, each containing a small square of its complementary colour.

Mixing two complementary colours will eventually give you a grey or brown. The resulting colour will usually be more interesting than a manufactured one from a tube. An orange (or orange-brown such as burnt sienna), when mixed with a mid-blue, will give a wonderful range of greys that can be warm or cool depending on the ratio of orange to blue. To make them paler, simply add white. These greys and browns are termed 'neutrals', and are very useful.

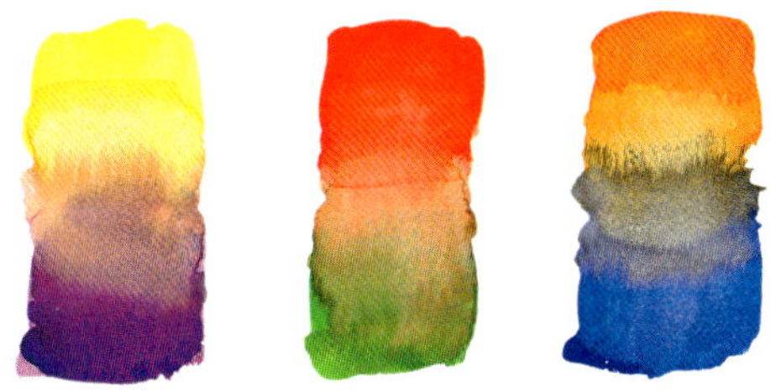

Greys and browns mixed from complementary colours.

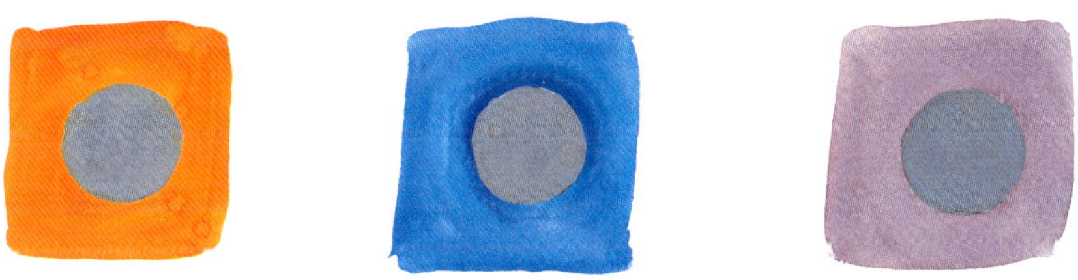

The interesting thing about colour is that it can appear to change, depending on what surrounds it, especially how dark or light the surround is.

Look at these circular grey shapes. They appear to differ subtly in tone. The one in the middle seems quite a bit lighter than the others, yet they are much the same colour. The reason for this optical illusion is the tone of the surrounding square. The blue square is easily the darkest, and so, by comparison, the grey looks lighter than the others, which have paler surrounds. It may also look slightly pinkish because it is affected by the coolness of the blue. When mixing colours, the relative 'tone,' that is, its darkness or lightness when compared to adjacent colours, is very important.

Tone

Tone is a subject best looked at first in shades of grey. Here are eight shades of grey made from a mix of burnt sienna and ultramarine blue. The lightest colour is white with a tiny touch of burnt sienna, the very dark tone on the right has had some Prussian blue added to darken it. You can see that they are lighter on the left and get progressively darker towards the right. The middle four are what we call mid-tones.

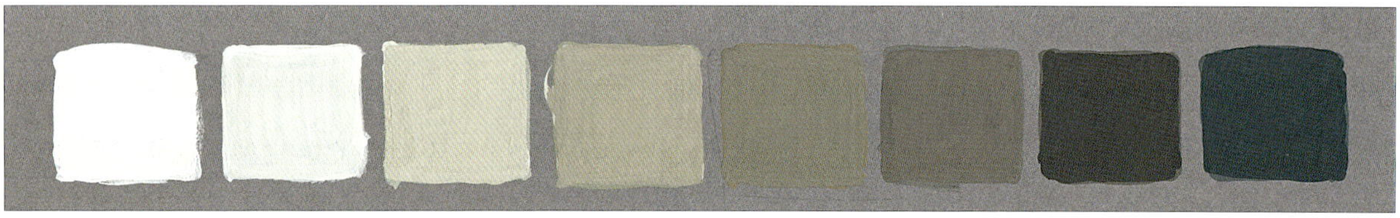

When painting with gouache, I tend to put the mid-tones in first, whatever the colour is, before moving on to the darker ones, and leave the very lightest, called highlights, until last. For instance, if you were painting a tree, you would paint the mid-green areas first, then the darker greens lower down and on the shadow side, then the pale greens of the sunlit side last of all. This is a very traditional way of working, especially with opaque mediums like gouache.

Every colour has a tonal range, from dark to light. If you cannot see tones easily (most people have a problem to start with), screw up your eyes and squint at them. That has the effect of reducing the number of tones you can see, and simplifies the contrasts.

It is very good practice to paint a tonal study like the one opposite every so often because it makes you appreciate how important the subject is. Look at the painting, which was made using the eight shades of grey described above. Why does the distant house at the top stand out from the background? The answer is because it is paler. Why does it look further away than the house with the steps? Because the house with the steps has more contrast around it, and is brighter.

Everything in this image relies on tone for clarity. Remember this for paintings you do in the future. You may do a painting that does not quite work, but perhaps you cannot figure out why. Before you start worrying about the colour or shapes of things, check your tones. That is probably where the problem is! I teach hundreds of classes every year and I am often asked, 'What's wrong with my painting?' The answer is usually a tonal one.

There is another element in this image that makes it work, and that is called 'colour temperature'. Look at the painting again, and compare the colour of the wall on the left of the road with the wall on the right. What do you see? The left one looks warm, with a hint of pink, and the right one looks cooler, in shadow, with a hint of blue. We can use temperature to create light and shade but, more importantly, we can use it to create the illusion of distance. This is where our colours start to become very exciting!

Opposite

A tonal study using the eight shades of grey shown above.

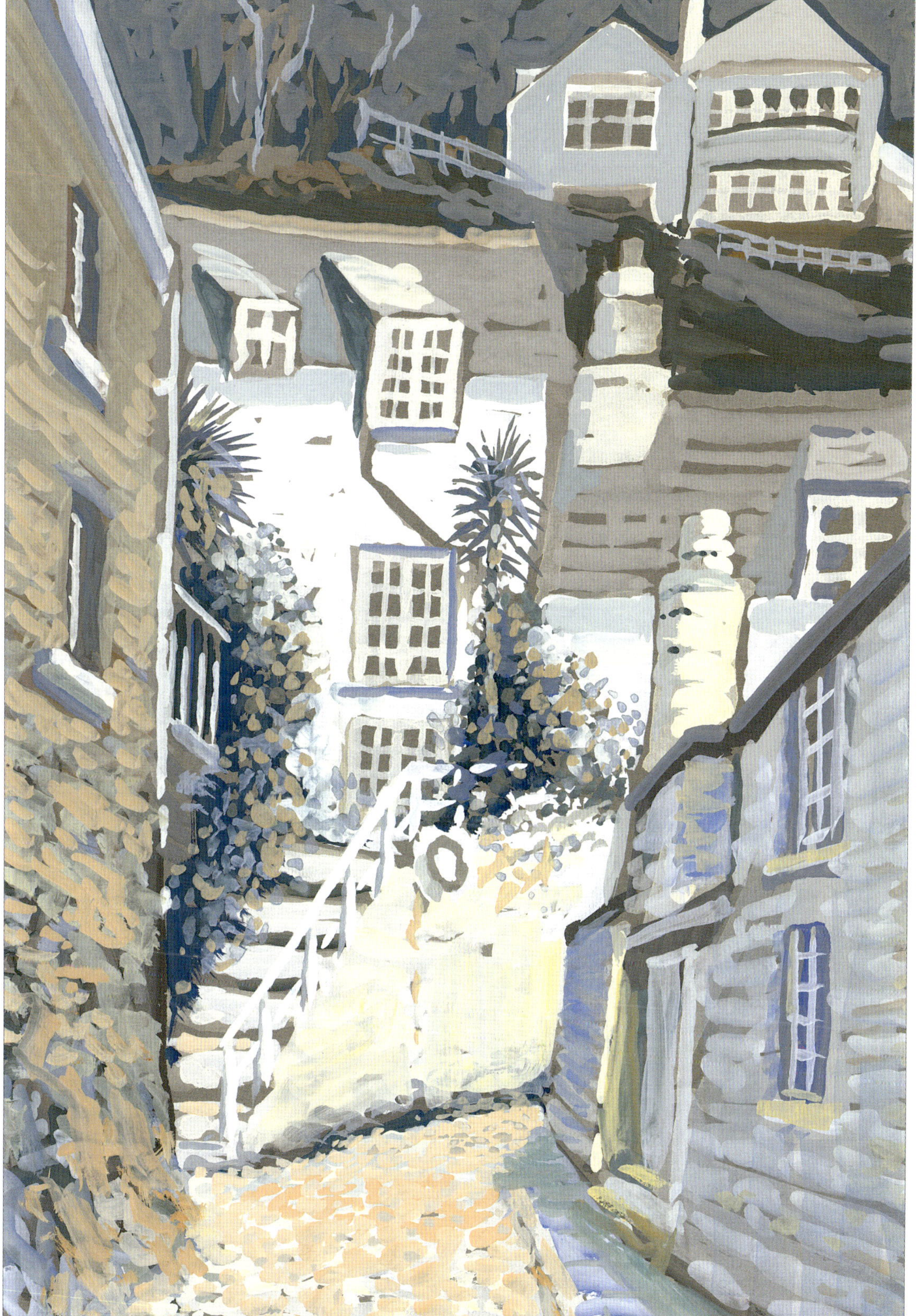

Three elements of a painting

A painting, even a relatively simple one like 'Dartmoor Cottage' shown opposite, is quite a complicated combination of several elements. The elements are tone, line and colour. We will find it easier to understand if we separate these areas and look at them individually, in order to see how a painting is made and the various decisions that have to be made during the process.

Tone, as we have already seen, is an important way of defining objects. It can tell us if something is in front of or behind something else. It is useful to explore tone in little pencil sketches, called thumbnail sketches, to help us plan a painting. Tone is about comparison; what is lighter or darker.

We can see that the cottage is much lighter than the trees behind it and a bit lighter than the ground in front of it, and the roof is slightly lighter than the distant hill. The right-hand side of the building is darker than the front, making it look solid, and we can tell where the sun is coming from. In other words, we have made the cottage stand out and look three-dimensional, purely by using tone.

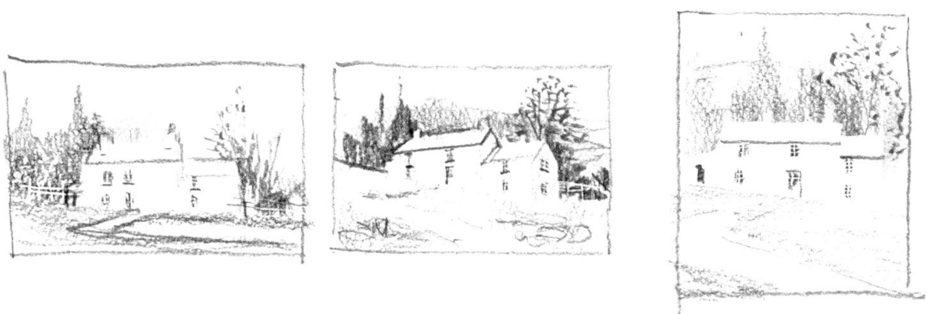

These little pencil sketches helped me decide where to put the different tones of the painting. Remember, to make something stand out, make it lighter or darker than its surroundings. The greater the contrast, the more it will stand out.

Line can be various things: the edge of a tonal area, where one colour joins another or a change in texture. All of these can create a line. Pathways, hedges, rivers, fences and rooftops all are linear. The important thing is that the viewer's eye will be attracted along a line. In other words, we can control the way someone sees our painting. The best paintings lead the eye around, in a sort of circuit, in such a way that the main parts of the image are connected. The ineffective paintings are the ones that have several different areas of interest, but with no connection between them.

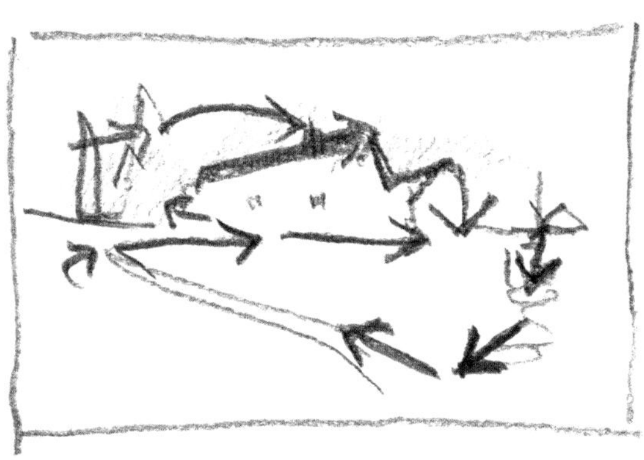

This little diagram shows where the viewer's eye should travel when looking at the painting. The difficult bit is the far right-hand side, where the fence finishes and the light building stands. I have added a few light-coloured boulders to help lead the eye down to the pathway.

Colour imparts the mood or atmosphere of a painting. A good painting can show the time of day, the time of year or the weather, all by careful choice of colour. If you are working from photographs, it is very tempting to try to copy exactly the colours in the photograph. However, usually the colours can be improved by the artist. My advice is to decide on the kind of atmosphere or mood you want to express, and then think about what colours fit that mood. Strong, vibrant colours give a feeling of heat, movement or wild countryside, whereas pale, subtle ones evoke tranquil times of day, stillness and peace. Warm colours such as red, orange, brown or deep yellow tend to give an impression of nearness, while cool colours such as blue, pale green or pale lemon yellow tend to look further away.

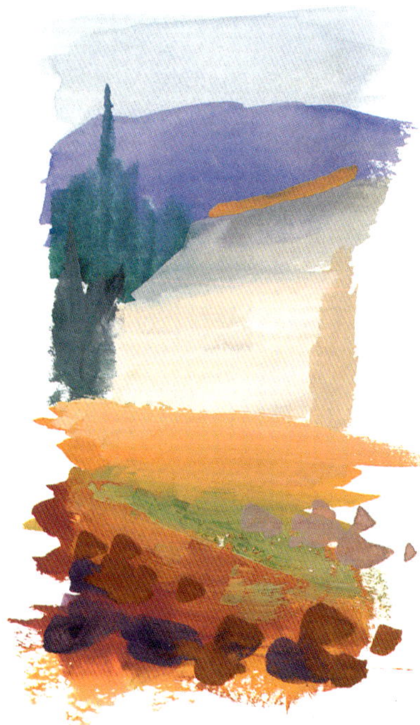

I often make little colour studies like this to get some idea of the colours to use. As you can see, the distance is blue, so that it recedes, the dark pine trees make the cottage stand out, and the foreground looks near because it is orange and brown, with red touches. In the main this is an orange and blue colour scheme. If you look at the colour section on pages 12 and 13, you will see that this is a complementary colour composition. If you put complementaries together like this, the end result is nearly always attractive.

Dartmoor Cottage
330 x 235mm (13 x 9¼in)

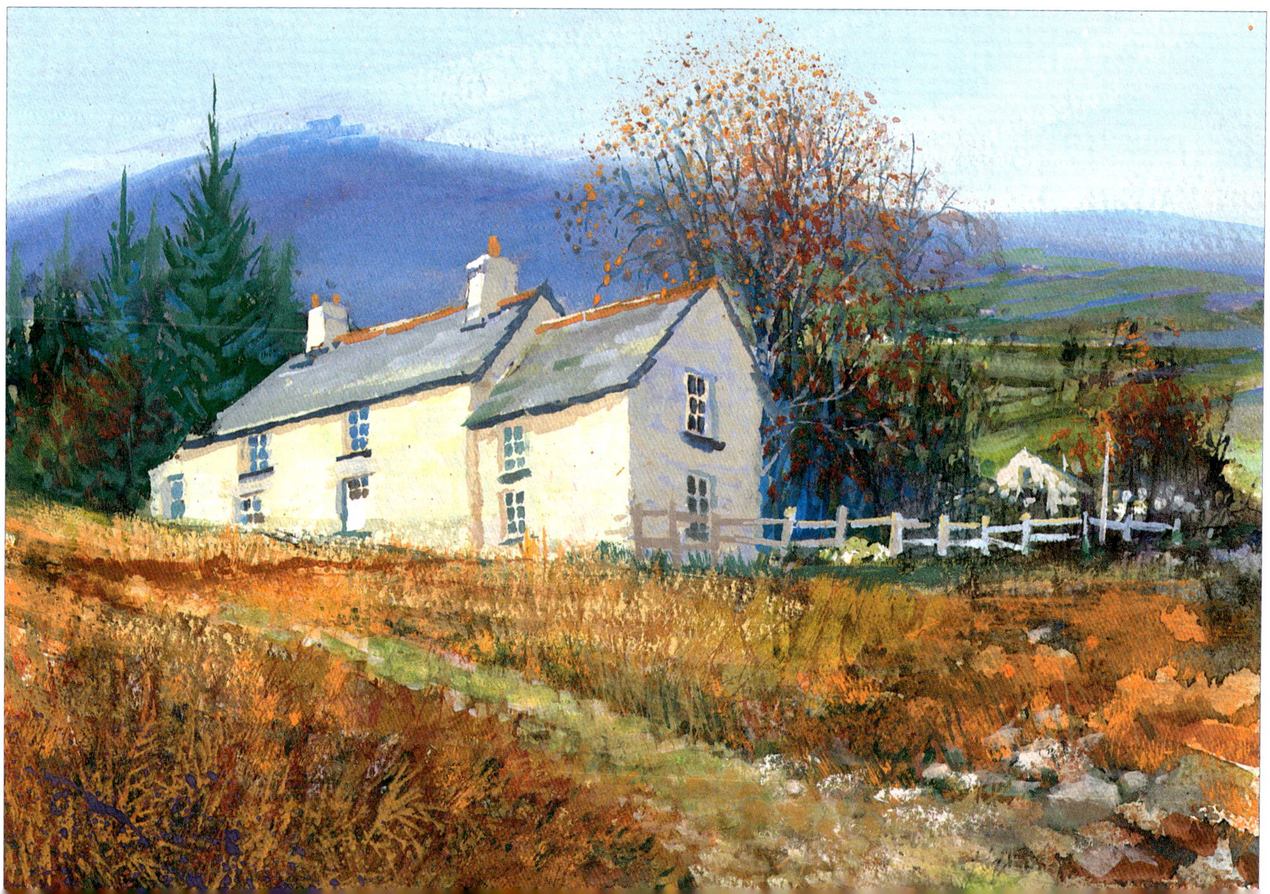

Composition

Composition is a vast subject, and many books have been devoted to it. It need not be that complicated to start with, though, and there are certainly some easily applied principles that you can use straight away. Take note of these, and your paintings will be improved immeasurably.

Choice of subject

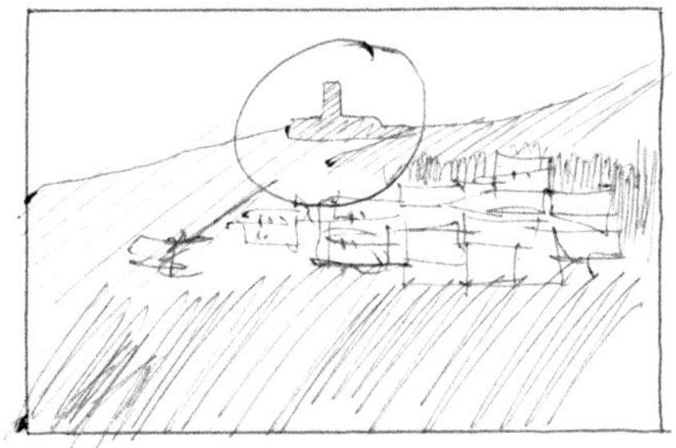

Have a clearly defined subject, or focal point. There may be more than one subject, but you should ensure that one is the main focus of attention, as in this sketch.

Placement

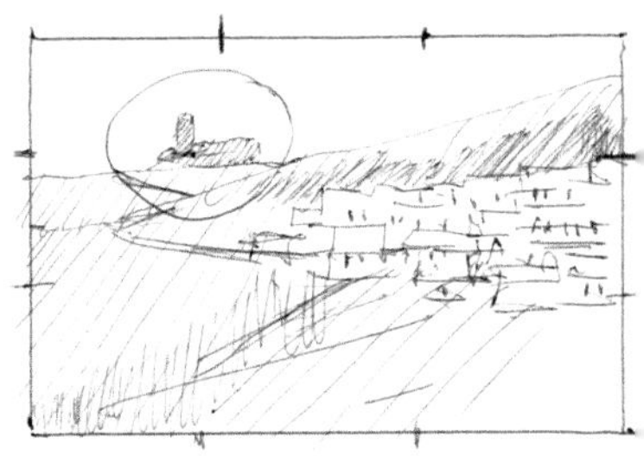

The cardinal rule here is never put the main subject or focal point right in the middle of the painting. It is so tempting to do this that you have to concentrate on planning in order to avoid it. The best way of planning is to use little thumbnail sketches like the one shown on the right. So, where to put the subject? Rather than placing the subject in the centre, arrange the image so that it falls roughly a third in from the sides or a third from the top or bottom. I often put little marks in these positions, on the edge of my thumbnail sketches, to remind me. Whatever else you do, this will ensure your work does not look boring or static.

Making connections

For simplicity's sake we can divide a painting into sections: distance – the furthest away from the viewer; middle distance – somewhere quite a bit nearer; and foreground – very close. To make our painting work, there should be links between each section; something to carry the eye from one part to another.

Simplification by omission

Basically, if it is not important, leave it out! Anything that does not support or enhance the subject should be considered dispensable. The best way to do that is to imagine what the painting would look like without it. If the image does not make sense without it, it stays: if the painting would still be good without it, consider leaving it out. All the great artists have used the art of simplification in this way. Another way of simplifying is to reduce the amount of detail. When painting a group of buildings, as in the Andalucian village scene shown opposite, you can leave out most of the windows and doors, while still achieving the desired effect.

Combining images

In this painting, of Al Monaster in Southern Spain, the subject is the tower on the hill. The mass of whitewashed cottages is a secondary subject, and the gate, fence and foliage in the foreground form an introduction, to lead the eye into the scene. All of these images exist. In reality, however, they are not in a position where you can see them all together. In other words I have combined three images to make an attractive scene. Many famous artists over the centuries have combined images like this to make stunning paintings. Our job is not to copy, but to make attractive images.

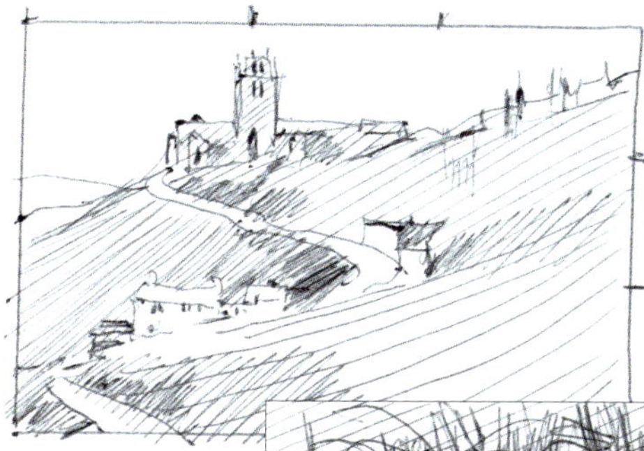

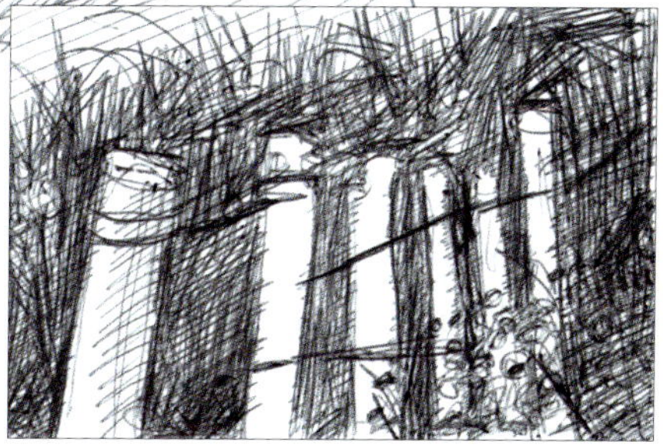

Al Monaster, Spain
340 x 265mm (13½ x 10½in)

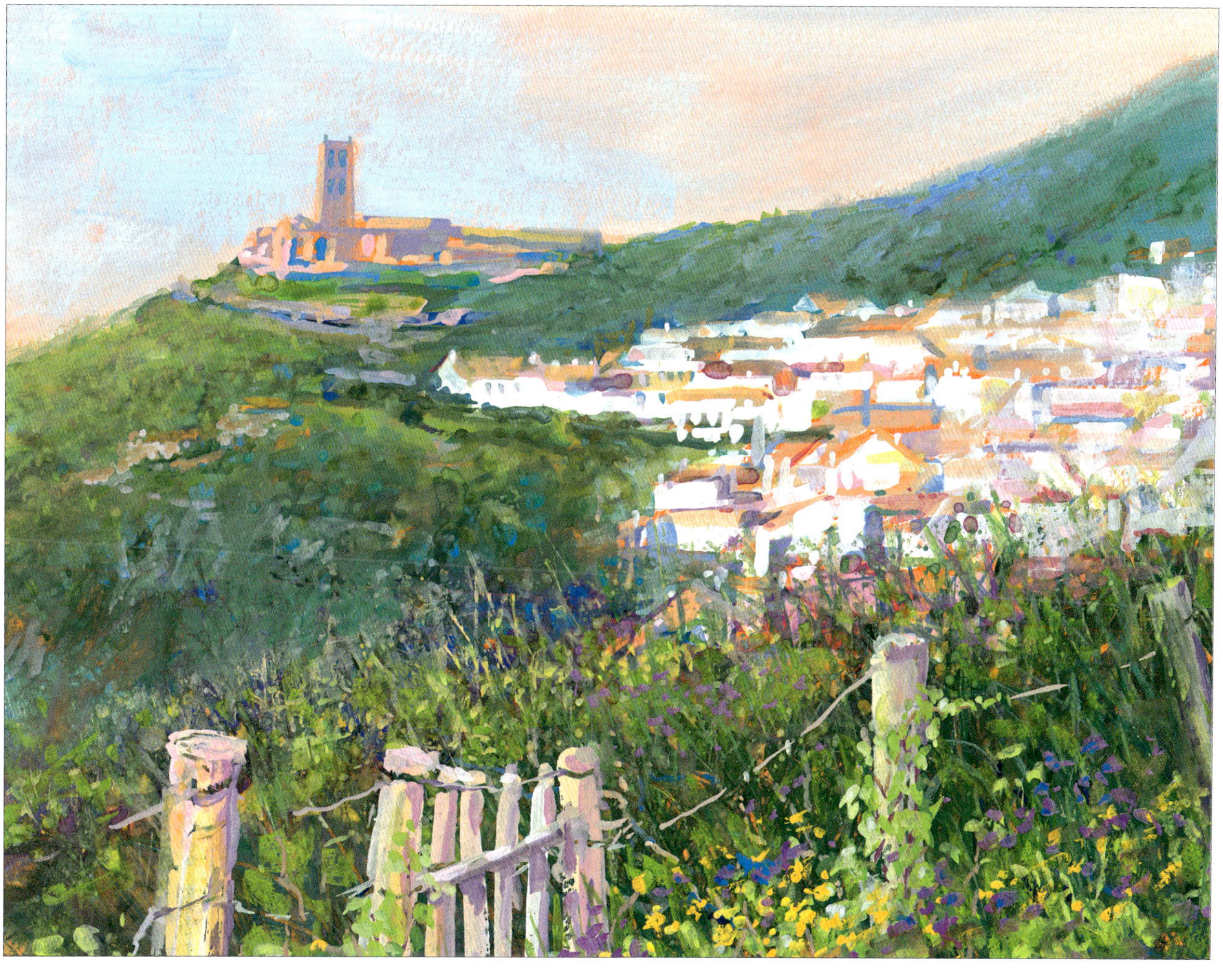

Techniques

All these creative methods work well with gouache. It is best to practise them on scrap paper before trying them on a painting, and experiment with various thicknesses of paint and a range of brushes and tools; only by trial and error will you find what works best. Also, note how the colours dry. Most gouache paints dry slightly darker, although on dark board it may look as though they are drying lighter. Mix some paint, apply it to white paper and then dry it using a hairdryer. Then put a touch of the wet paint on top and see the difference.

Wet in wet

This technique is the same as the traditional watercolour one and is useful for the soft, fuzzy edges for clouds, or to impart distance. You need to thin the paint slightly more than usual and quickly apply one colour adjacent to or on top of the other. The gouache should spread in a most attractive way. If it does not work, the paint is too thick or you have allowed too much time between one colour and the next. Sometimes it helps to wet the paper first, and in very hot weather I have had to wet the paper, and then put a sheet of wet blotting paper underneath it to keep it moist while painting.

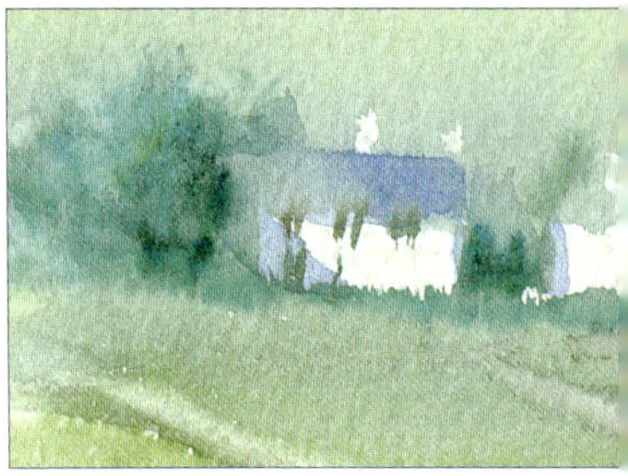

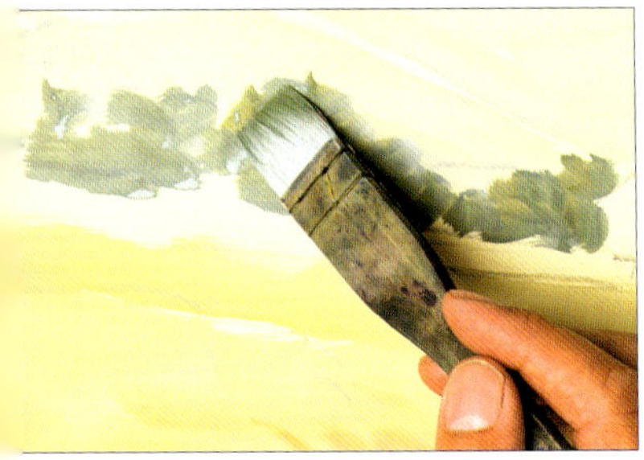

Wet on dry

This is useful anywhere where you want crisp edges and unblended colour, with separate brush strokes showing. This is one of the classic gouache techniques, and its effect can be very vibrant. A wonderful shimmering effect can be built up by placing strokes of different colours next to one another or one over the other, without blending or softening the edges. Since it is an opaque medium, gouache can be applied dark on light or the other way round.

Masking

Masking can be used to good effect, especially on watercolour paper. The method consists of applying masking fluid – a liquid similar to rubber solution – to small areas that need to be left white. The fluid is left to dry thoroughly. The whole area is then overpainted with a darker colour, and when the paint is dry, the masking fluid is removed to show the white paper, which gives strength to any colours that are applied on top. This technique is familiar to watercolourists, who like to use the white of the paper, and works equally well for gouache.

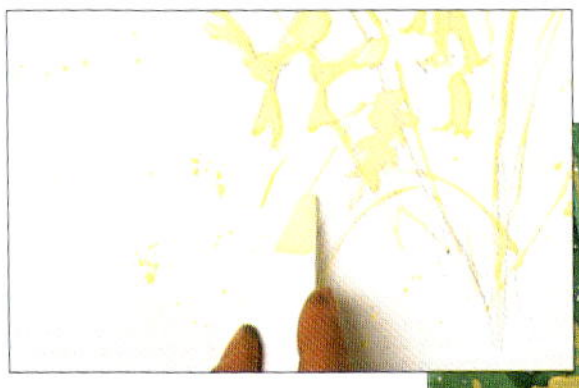

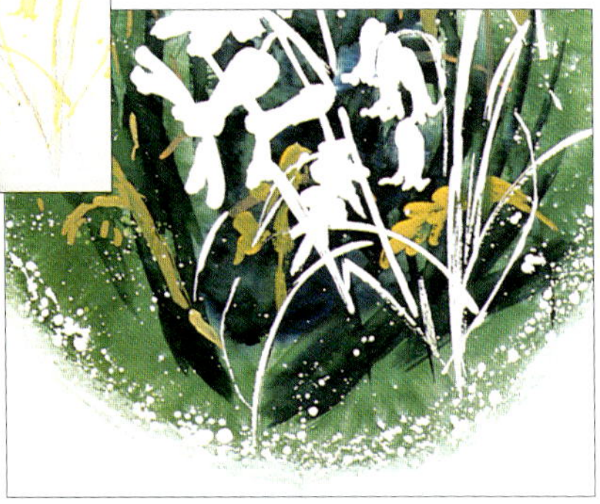

Lifting out

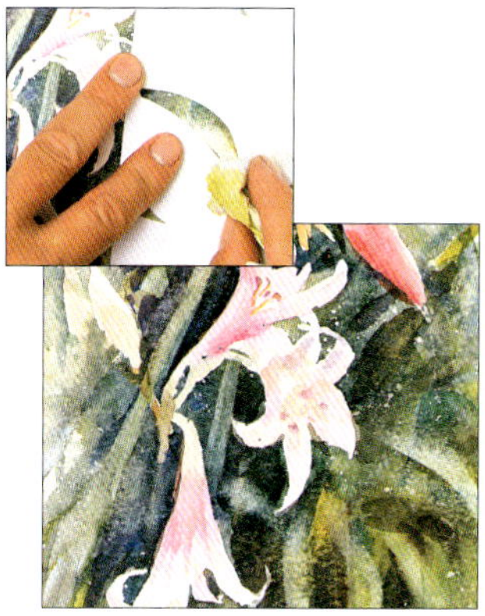

This relies on the removable nature of the paint. Most colours can be lifted out with a damp cloth, leaving a paler version behind, or all the colour can be removed. Shapes can be created by cutting negative shapes such as leaves out of paper, and gently rubbing through these stencils. This works best on watercolour paper, especially the heavier types.

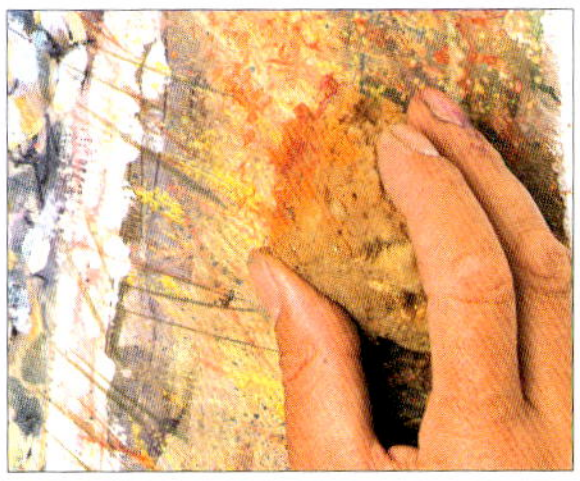

Sponging

Texture is a fundamental part of my gouache painting, especially in the foreground. I use natural sponges, dipped in one or more colours, to apply a stippled effect where I want to create a look of rough ground, scrubby foliage, or leaves. Other tools such as crinkled paper or folded card can be used to create a variety of effects.

Sgraffito

Sgraffito is a natural technique for oil painters to use, but is not common among watercolourists. It works by scraping back through a wet colour with a pointed stick, the end of a knife or something similar to expose the colour beneath. You must use this technique quickly – within seconds of applying the paint – otherwise it will be too dry to work. Sgraffito creates wonderfully spontaneous-looking marks which are very useful in the foreground to add texture.

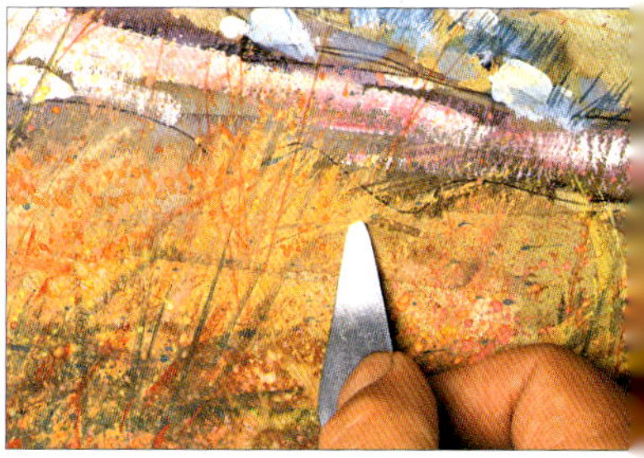

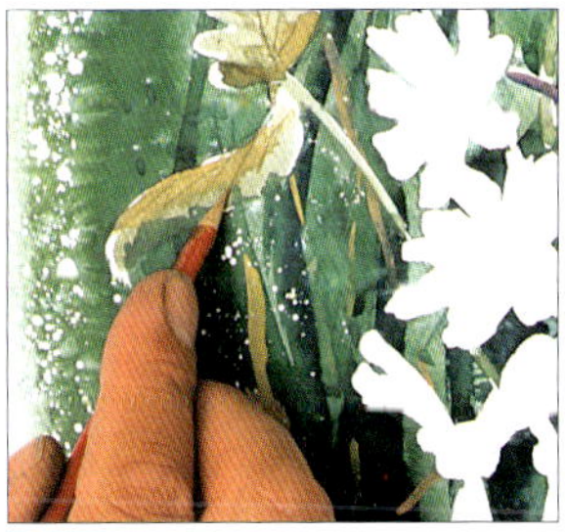

Indenting

Indenting is related to sgraffito. It entails using a sharp implement to push into the surface of an area of wet paint. The indentations caused then fill with paint and dry a different colour from the rest. I find it useful for creating veins on close-up leaves, implying twigs or branches, and putting ripples on water. Remember, you have to be quick, so have everything ready before you start painting.

Spattering

Spattering is a wonderful, loose way of putting texture into a painting. Stones on a path, cobbles, leaves and more can be applied in this way. It works best using a household paintbrush (preferably a new one, solely for this purpose), well loaded with runny paint. Pulling the bristles back, away from the painting, then quickly releasing them will cause an irregular spray of droplets. The rest of the painting should be protected by old newspapers or scrap paper, as you do not have much control over where the paint goes. Great fun!

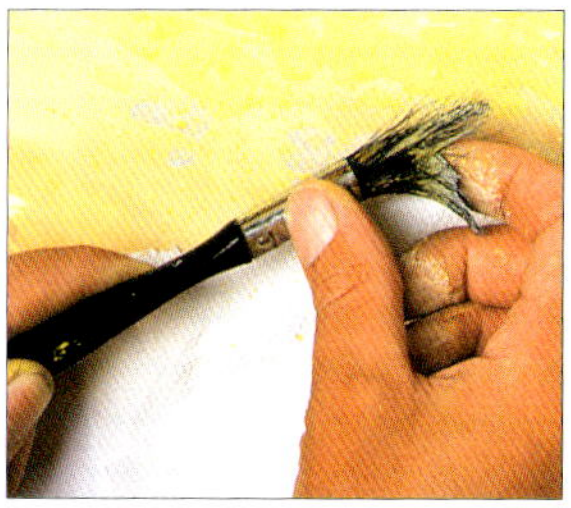

Landscape

This is a simple landscape, very satisfying to do. It is taken from my sketchbook, and uses a very limited palette of four colours and white.

The image is a house on Dartmoor near where I live, and where I used to play as a child. It was derelict then, and I imagined that one day I might buy it and renovate it. When I walked past and discovered someone had bought it and was working on it, I was quite annoyed! It would have been a very impractical place to live though: no decent road for a mile, no electricity, no running water. But great for getting away from it all!

You will need

- Cream or yellow card, 420 x 295mm (16½ x 11⅝in)
- 2B pencil
- Colours: primary blue, lemon yellow, alizarin crimson, burnt sienna and permanent white
- 2.5cm (1in) hake brush, no. 6 and no. 12 round brushes, a household paintbrush
- Kitchen paper

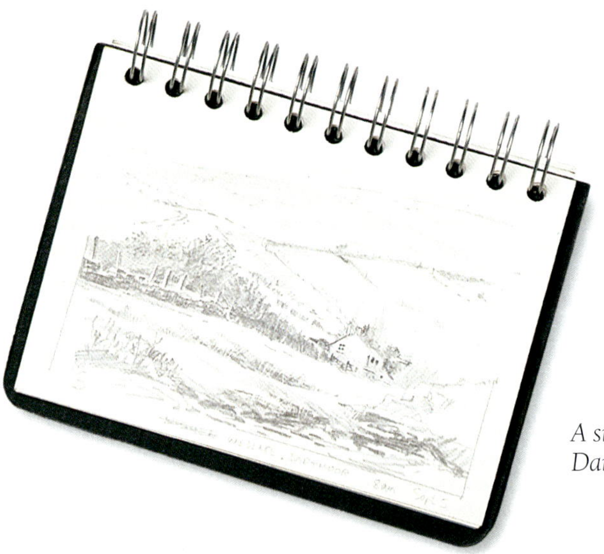

A simple sketch of a Dartmoor farm.

1. Draw the scene on the card.

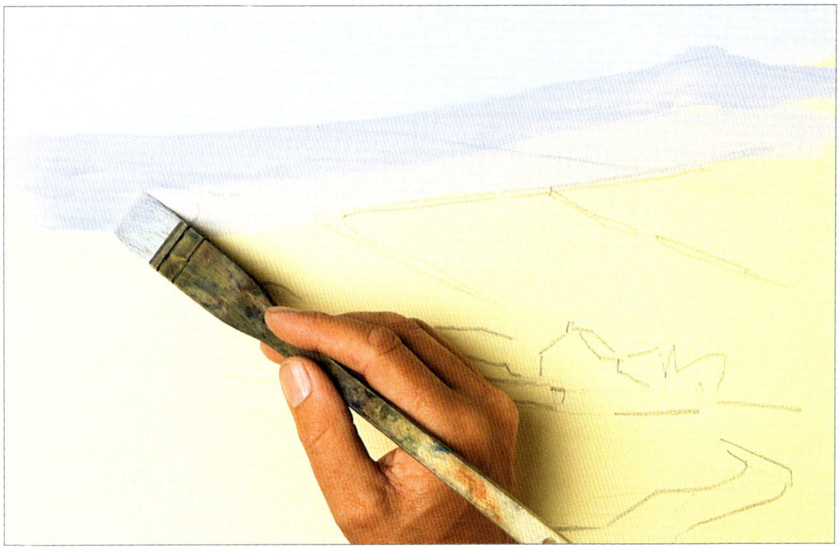

2. Block in the sky area using the hake brush and a mix of white with a little primary blue, and a touch of burnt sienna to grey it slightly. Use a little more primary blue in the mix, with a touch of alizarin crimson, for the distant hills.

3. Add lemon yellow and primary blue to white, with a tiny bit of burnt sienna, to block in the fields in a thin coat of grey-green.

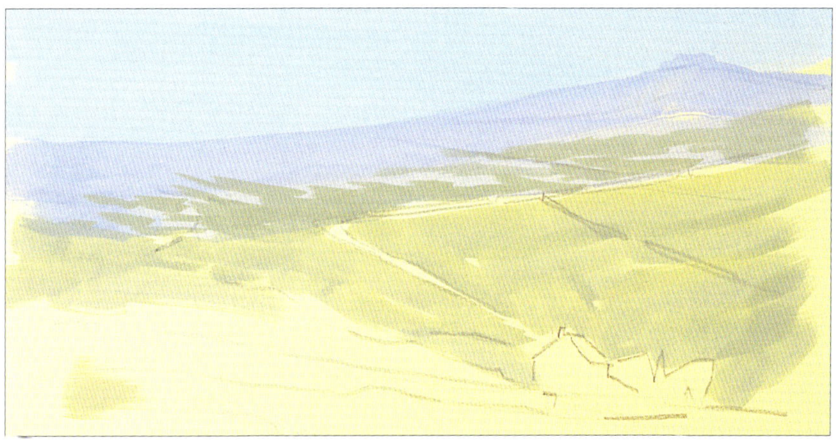

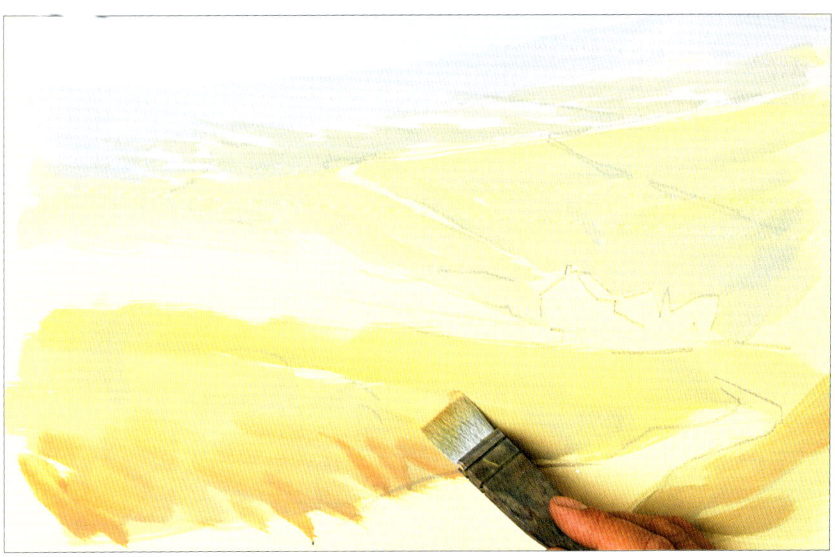

4. Mix a similar green for the area nearer the foreground, but make it darker and warmer by adding a little burnt sienna. Add more burnt sienna for the foreground, making diagonal strokes down to the path with the corner of the hake brush.

5. Mix lemon yellow with primary blue and burnt sienna with a hint of white to paint the darks behind the farmhouse and the rest of the hedge.

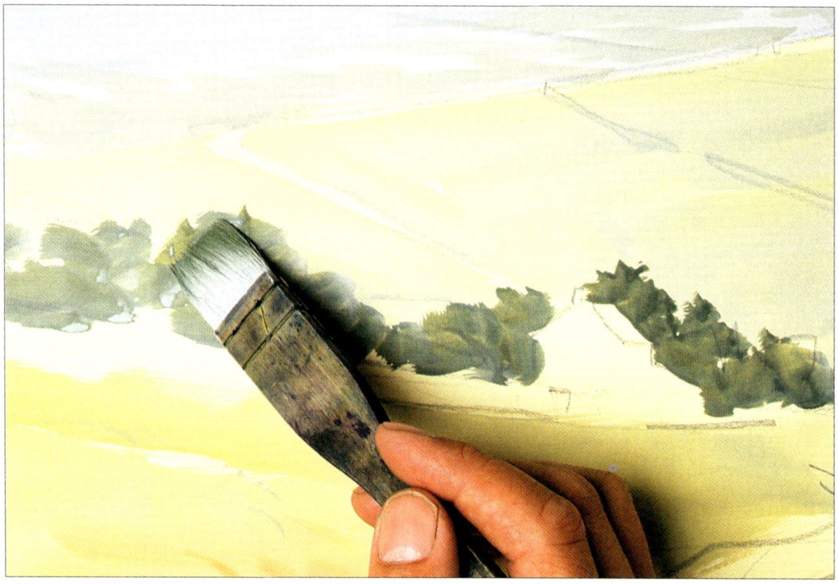

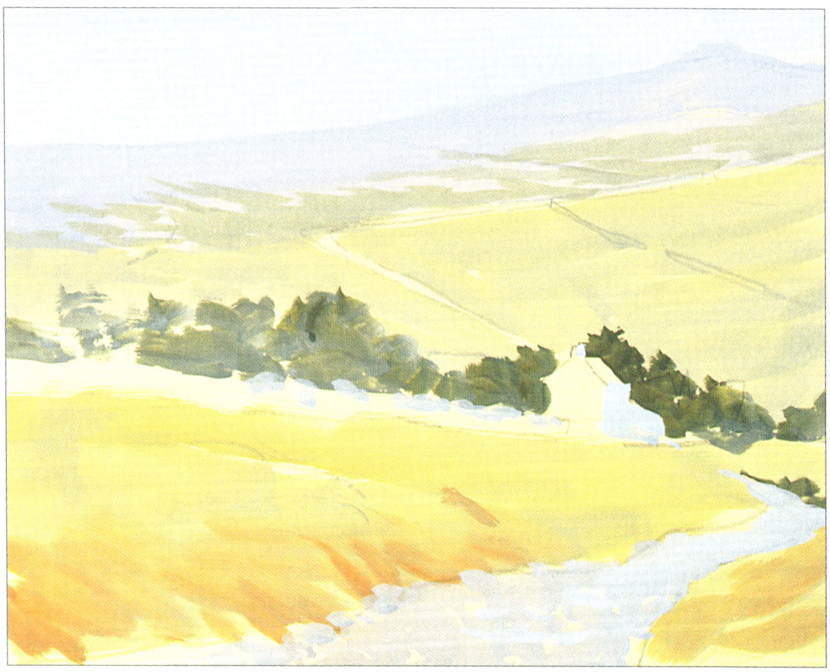

Note

Clean your brushes regularly as gouache leaves a heavy sediment and one colour could contaminate another. Make sure you change the water often.

6. Mix a warm grey for the pathway from burnt sienna, primary blue and white. Paint in a loose, irregular way with the corner of the hake brush so that the background colour shows through. Further away add more white and blue to create aerial perspective. Paint the top of the wall in the same colour where the light catches it. Use a similar grey, a little bluer, for the shadowed right-hand side of the house.

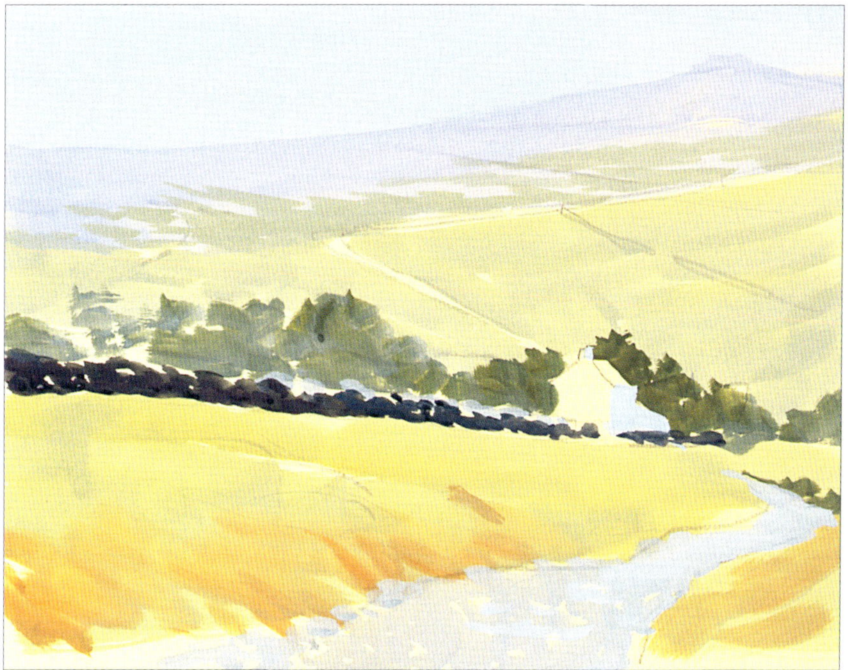

7. Paint the darks on the stone wall using burnt sienna with primary blue and a tiny bit of alizarin crimson, but no white. Allow touches of the board to show through in an irregular pattern. Add more blue in the distance so that it appears to recede. Near the house, add white to make the colour paler.

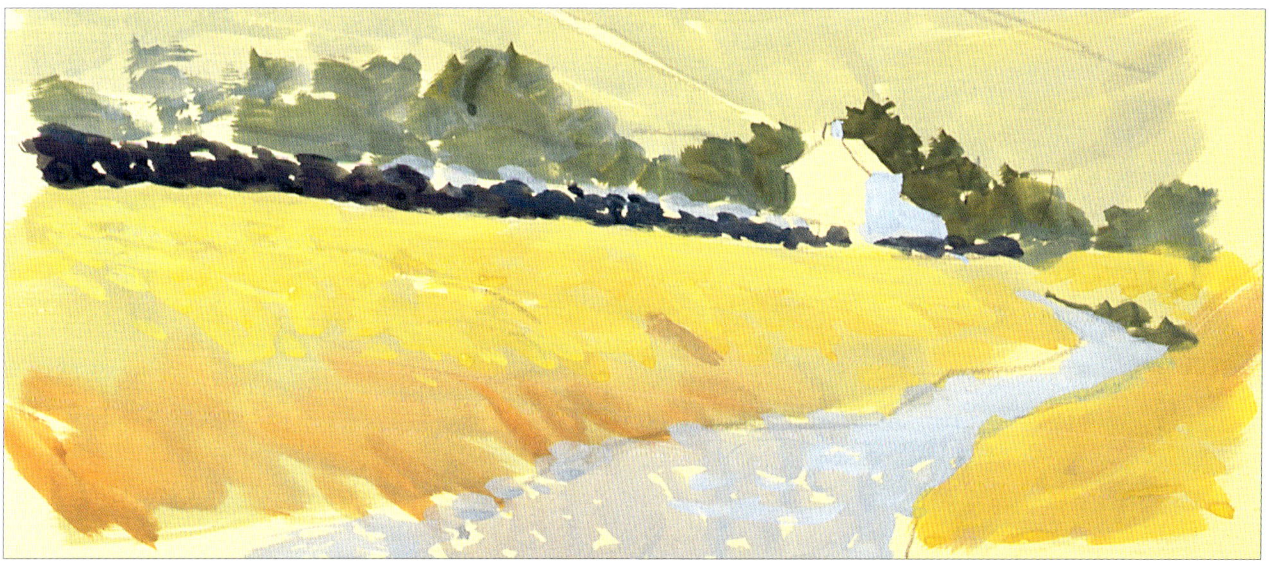

8. Mix lemon yellow, burnt sienna and white to make a pale brownish-yellow for the right-hand side of the pathway where it catches the sun. The mix should be thinned with water to make it semi-transparent. Add texture to the top of the bank and to the foreground right-hand corner with the same mix. Create texture by sweeping a relatively dry brush over the surface.

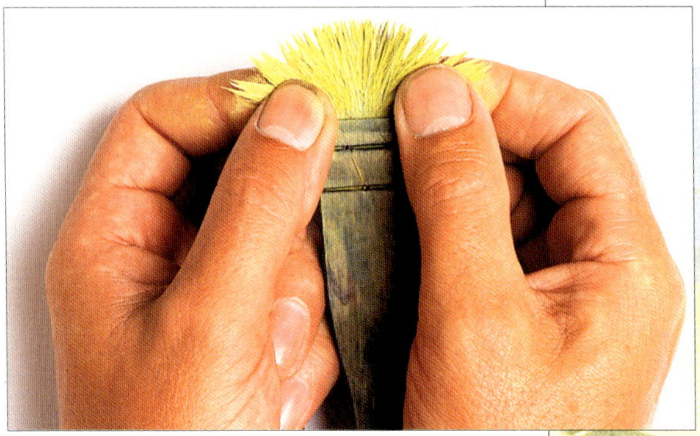

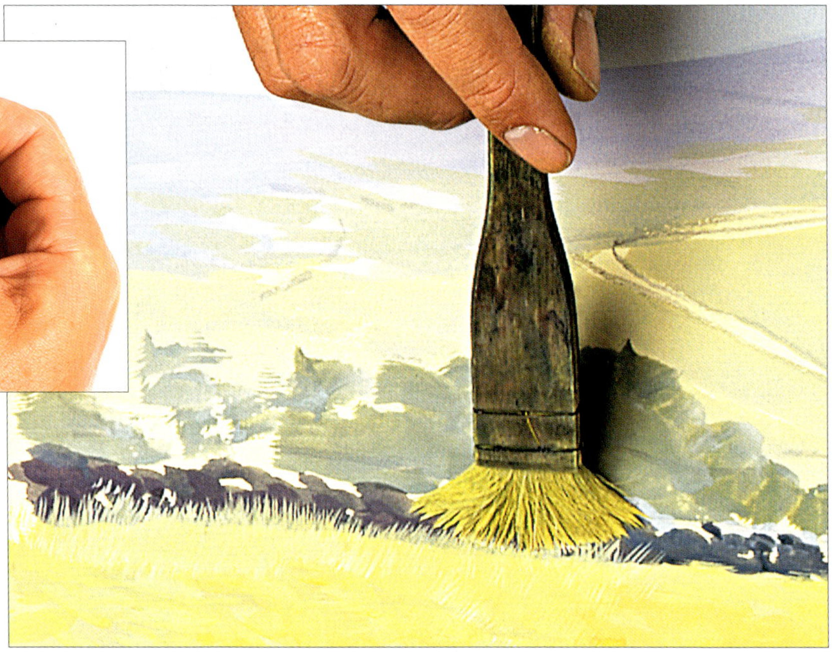

9. Take the hake brush and fan out the bristles as shown above. Use the brush to paint the grasses against the hedge using lemon yellow, a touch of primary blue and white.

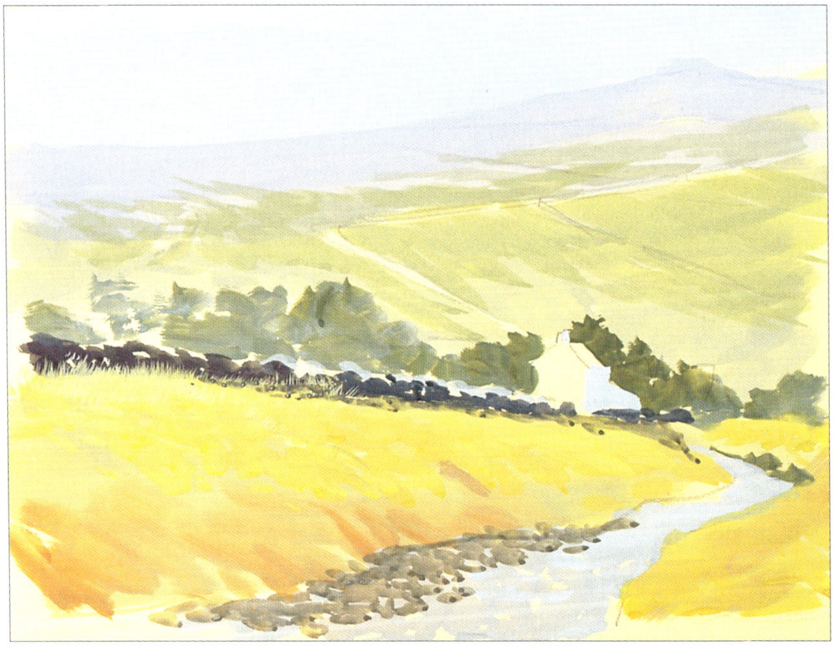

10. Mix lemon yellow, primary blue and white and rework the fields to vary the colour. Your brush strokes should run downhill with the land. Change to the no. 12 brush and shadow the left-hand edge of the pathway in a darker grey mixed from primary blue, burnt sienna and white. Mix a slightly bluer grey to paint the shadow under the stone wall.

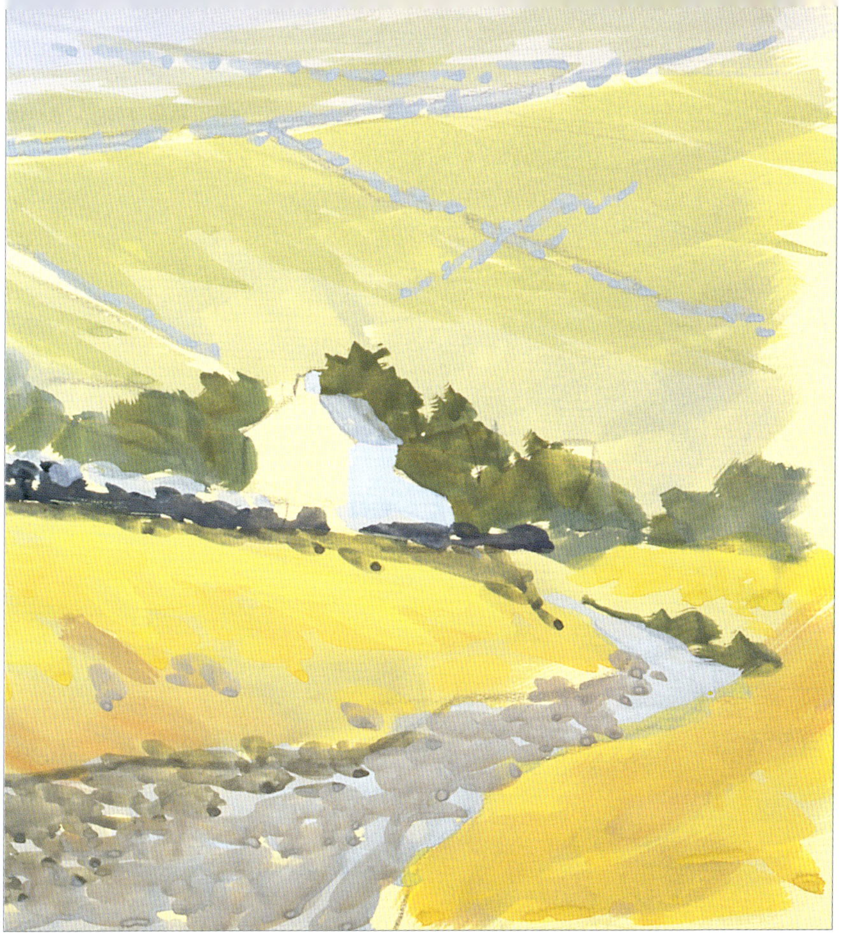

11. Paint the distant wall and the boulders on the moorland in a bluey grey, using broken lines. Pick out some stones at the top of the main wall with the same colour, and use it again on the shadowed side of the house's roof. Brown the mix with burnt sienna to paint stones in the path and the shadows of boulders near the foreground.

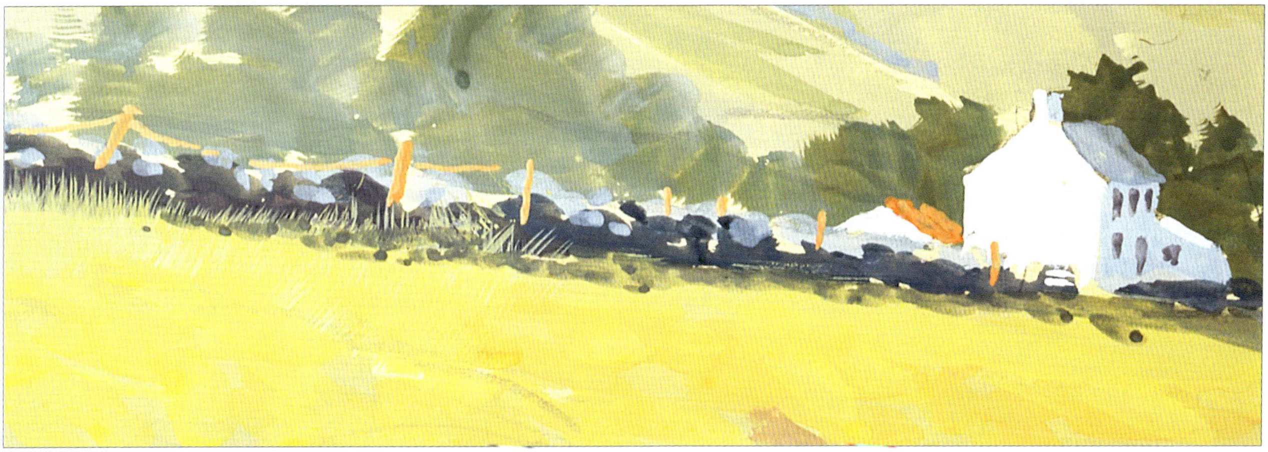

12. Mix white with a little burnt sienna to warm it, and use the no. 6 brush to paint the lit side of the cottage, adjusting its shape as you go. Paint the negative shape of the gate, and the light on the roof of the lean-to. Paint in the shed on the left of the house. Mix alizarin crimson, lemon yellow and white for the rusty colour of the shed roof, and use the same colour for the fence posts above the hedge. These should lean into the painting to lead the eye inwards. Paint in touches of the fence wire. Use the same brush with a dark grey mix to paint slits in the shadowed side of the house for windows.

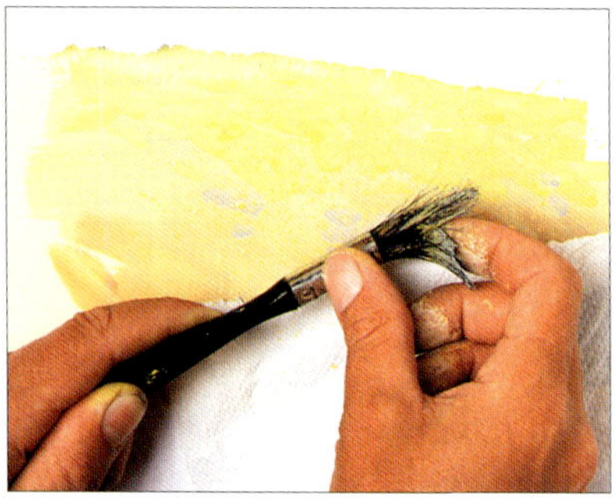

13. Make a pale orange mix from lemon yellow, alizarin crimson and white. Mask the area around the left-hand side of the path in the foreground using kitchen paper. Use a household brush to spatter the paint over this area.

The finished painting

355 x 270mm (14 x 10⅝ in)

At the final stage of the painting I added lights, using permanent white warmed with burnt sienna for the posts and the left-hand side of the stones in the wall. I also added highlights on the left-hand side of the boulders in the foreground and on the path.

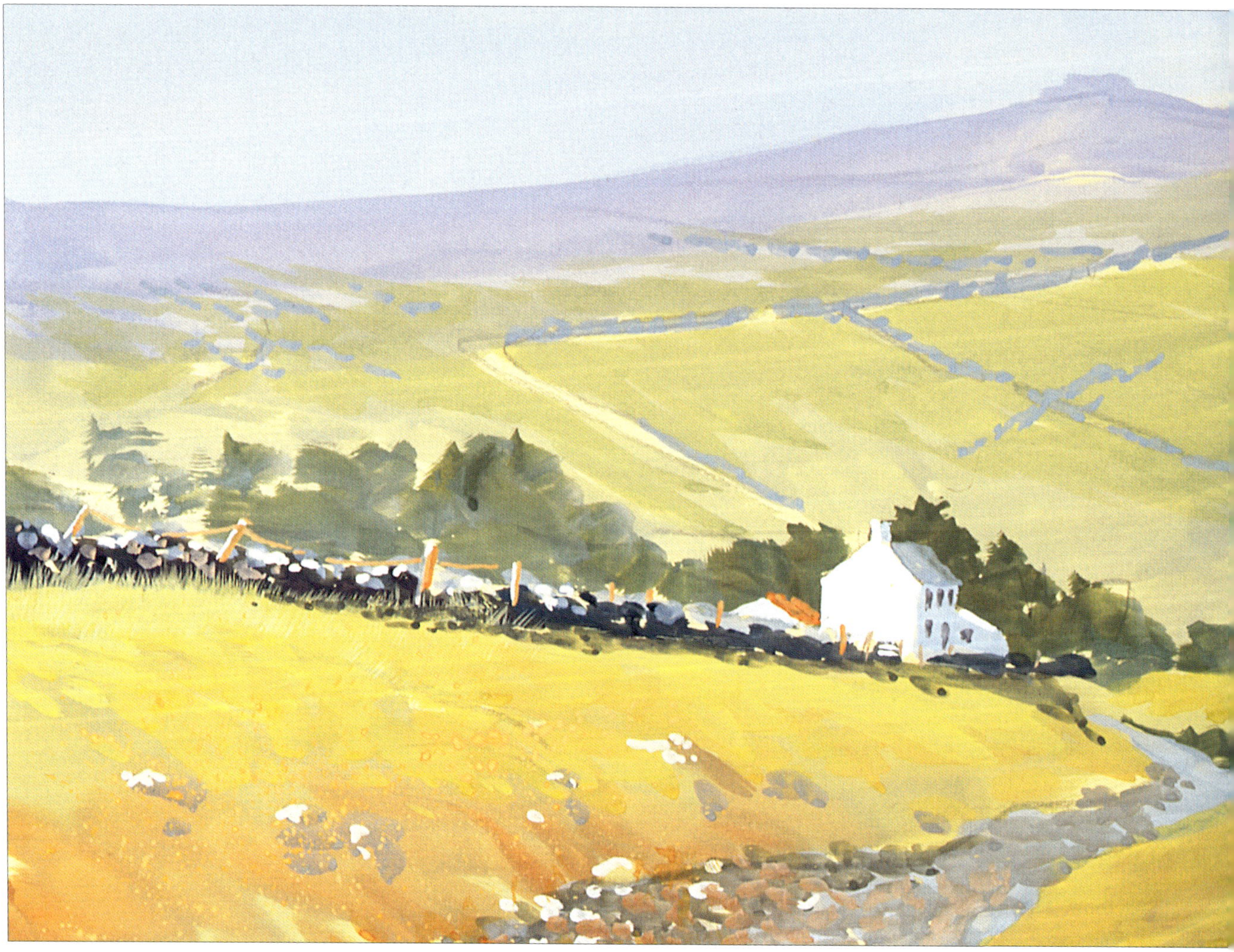

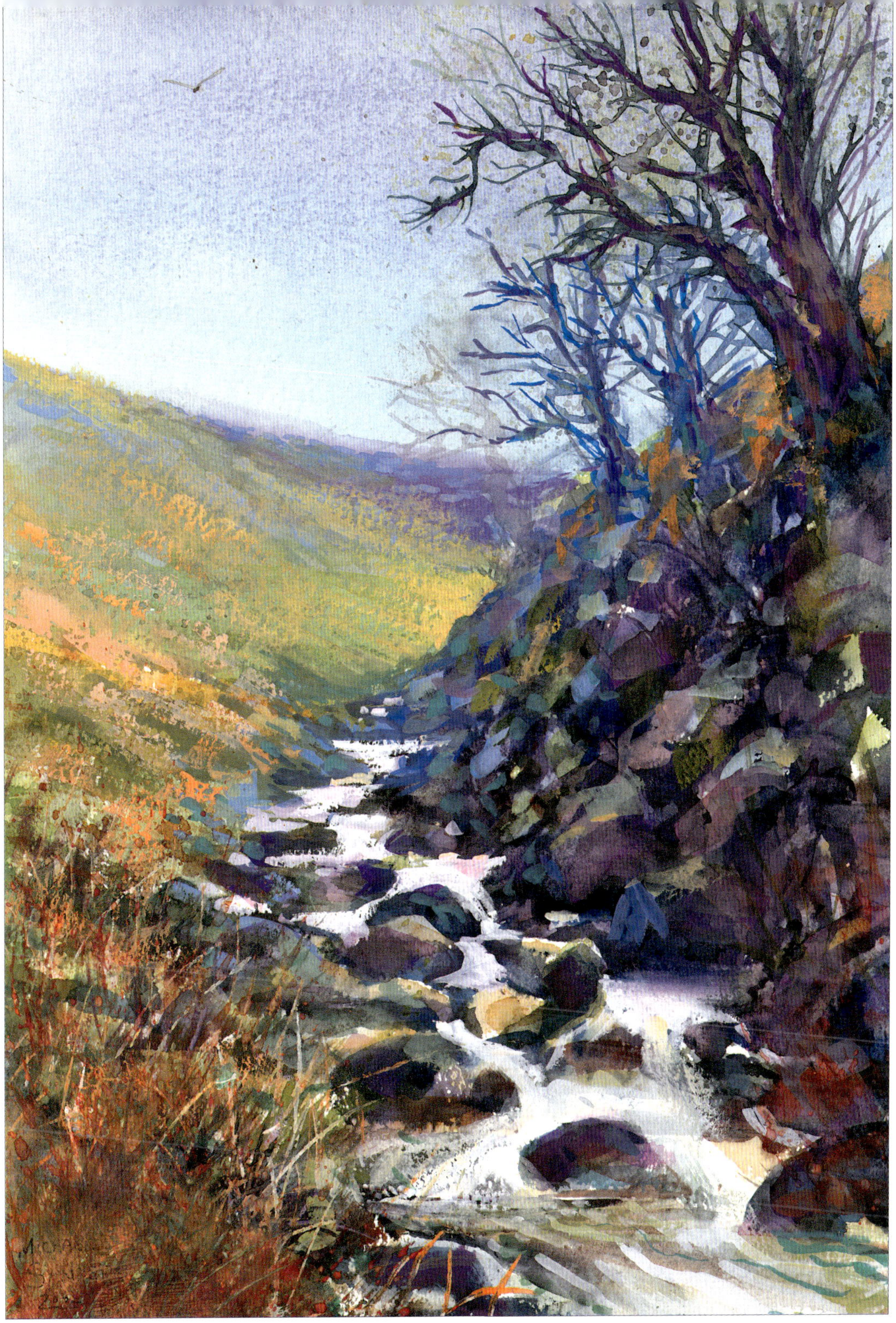

Tavy Cleave

240 x 340mm (9½ x 13⅜in)

This wonderful spot was painted using more or less the same colours as in the Landscape project. I used the angular nature of the hake brush to apply the boulders on the right, and a mix of sponging, spattering and sgraffito to paint the area on the left. The water was first painted a very pale green, and then white was applied once this had dried. I dropped additional colours into the tree trunks while they were still wet, and this has run and separated to good effect.

Ruined Andalucian Farmstead

530 x 360mm (21 x 14¼in)

Every year in spring and autumn, I go to Spain to tutor painting holidays. In the hot climate, gouache is an ideal medium to use since, if it dries too quickly, it can easily be re-wetted and made workable again. I took a party up into the hills in a four-wheel drive vehicle and we spent the day there – a wonderful experience. The old farm had been abandoned many years earlier due to the water source drying up. My painting was also drying up, and I had to wet it several times as I worked; the marks are visible as part of the finished image. Sometimes it is a temptation to 'tidy things up' when we get them home, but it is not always a good idea, as the spontaneity can get lost in the process. I am particularly fond of the spattered, sponged and scraped foreground in this painting.

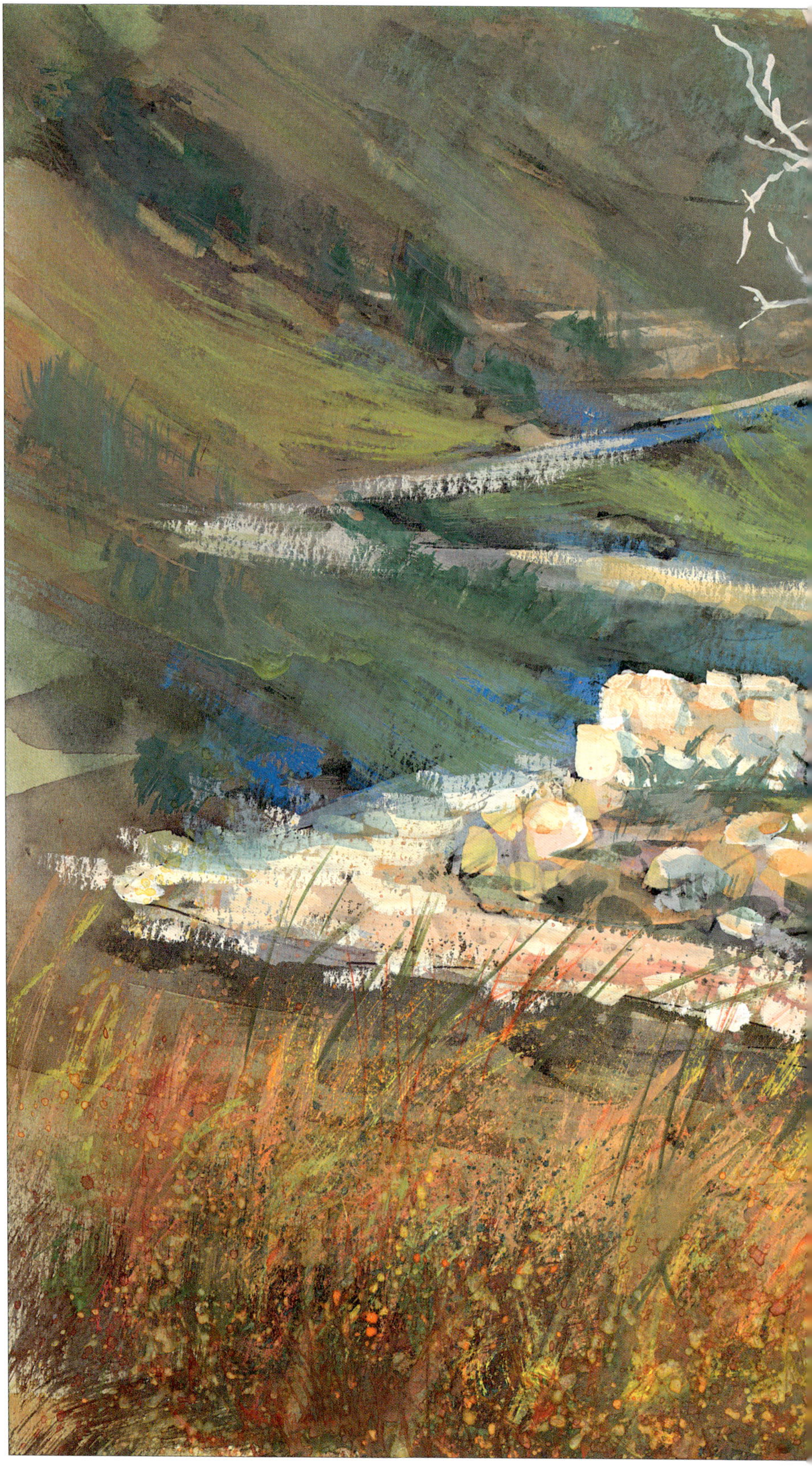

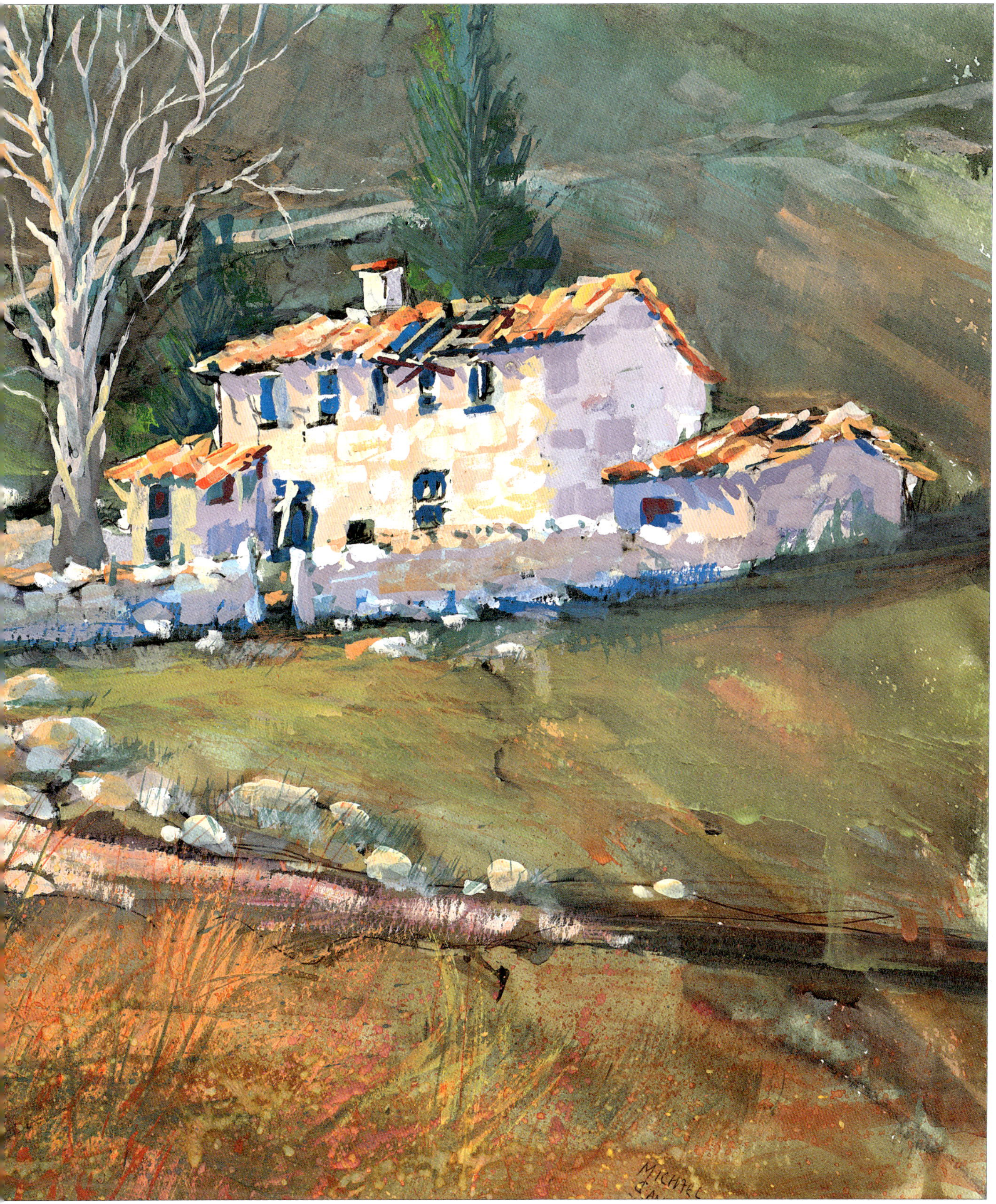

Flowers

This is a nice image that uses masking fluid to good effect. It is important when using this technique to allow plenty of time for the fluid to dry, or your brushes could be contaminated by it. When the painted background is dry, remove the dry fluid by rolling it off the surface with a piece of kitchen paper, rather than pulling it directly, to avoid tearing the paper. Paint along with this project, and then why not try a flower study of your own? Pale blooms on a dark background work well with this method.

You will need

Heavyweight watercolour paper
2B pencil
Masking fluid
Scrap paper
Masking tape
Colours: Prussian blue, sap green, Naples yellow, burnt sienna, ultramarine blue, azure blue, magenta, marigold yellow, flame red, permanent white and permanent yellow deep
Large hake brush, no. 10 and no. 12 round brushes, old brush with sharpened end
Kitchen paper
Stiff paper or thin card

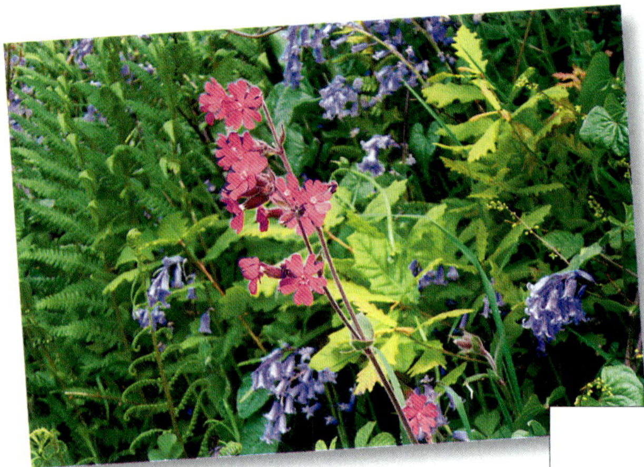

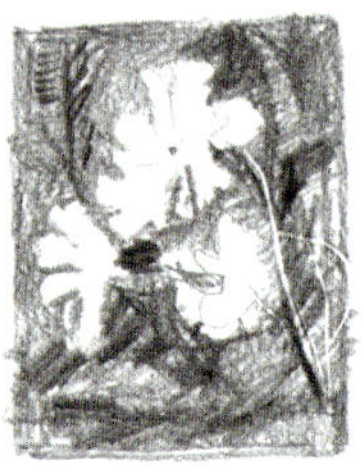

It is best to do a few thumbnail sketches to plan your painting. I have chosen the oval shape as a format.

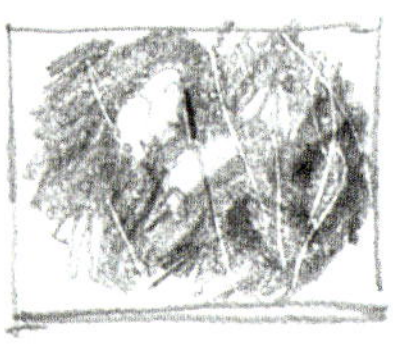

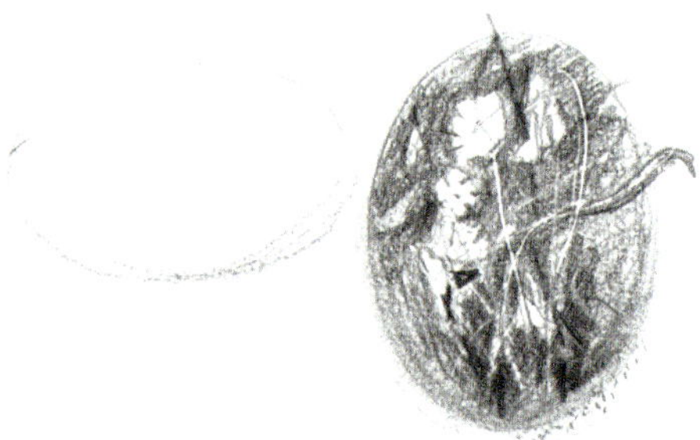

1. Make your sketch with lightly drawn lines using the 2B pencil.

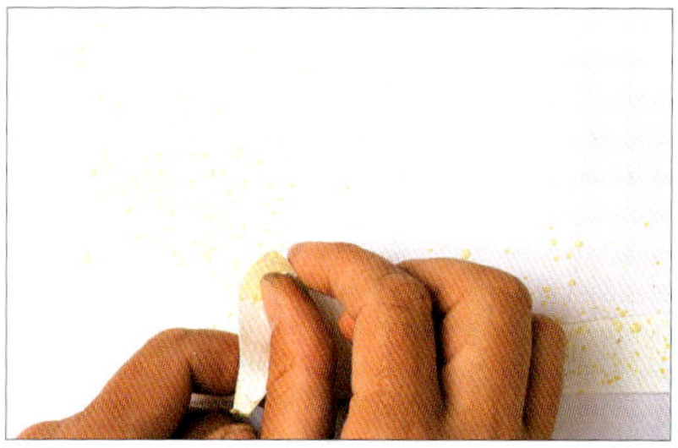

2. Cut an oval shape out of the scrap paper and lay it flat on the watercolour paper. This will form the shape of the oval vignette. Dip a piece of paper in masking fluid and flick the paper to spatter masking fluid over the edges of your oval shape. Practise the spattering technique on a separate piece of paper first. Make sure that enough masking fluid is applied to define the edge of the oval.

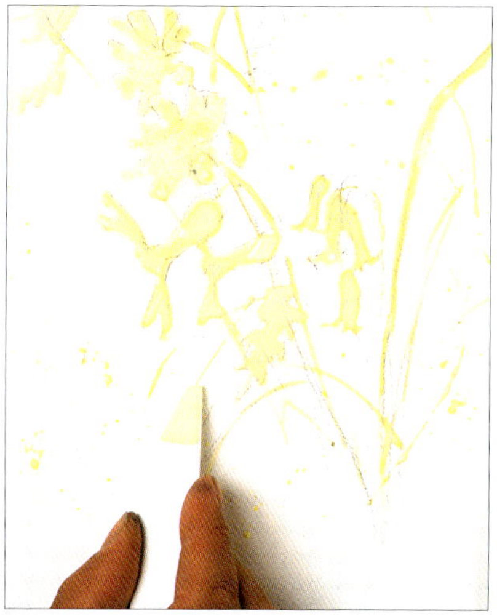

3. Using a pointed piece of stiff paper or thin card like a pen nib, draw in the flowers and leaves with masking fluid, then set it aside to dry.

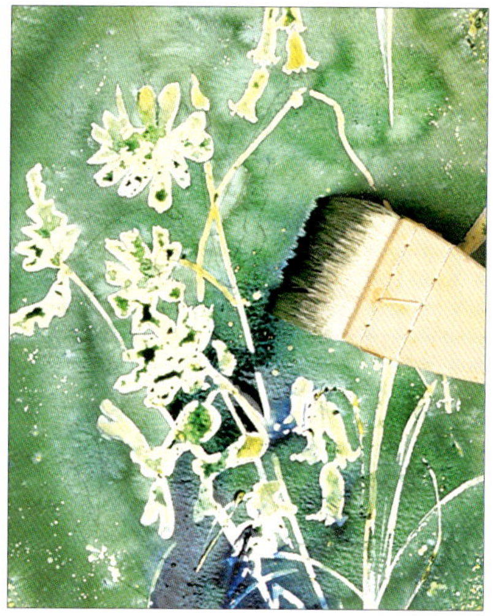

4. Take the hake brush and a mix of sap green and azure blue and paint over the whole oval area of masking fluid. Add more azure blue to paint the centre of the composition.

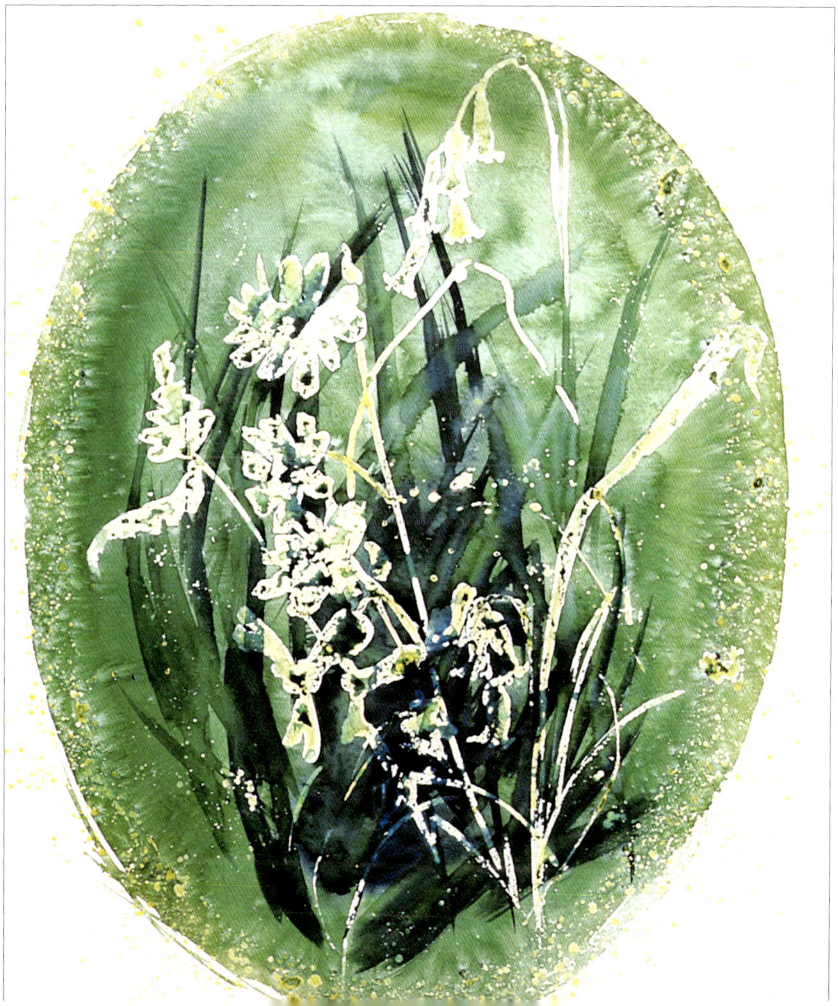

5. Use the tip of the hake brush to work the foliage in Prussian blue and sap green. The colours should be darker and bluer at the bottom to give the painting a base, and darkest behind the masked out areas, which will be light.

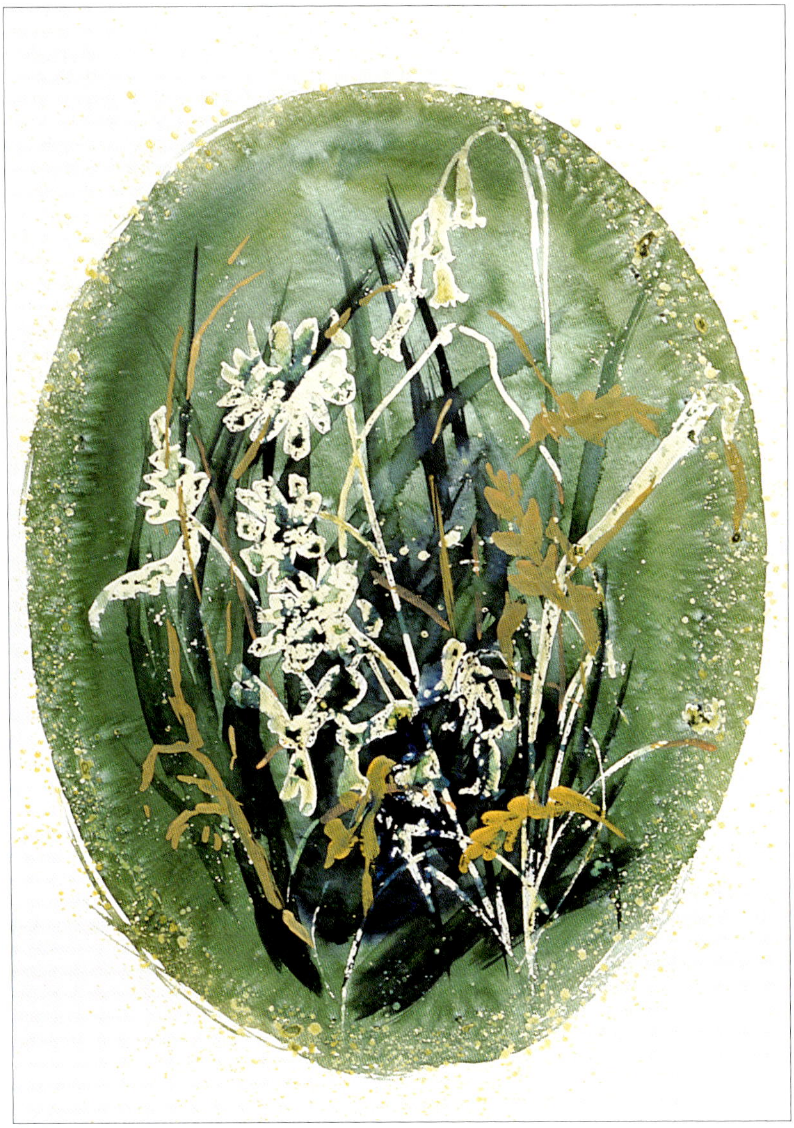

6. Mix Naples yellow and burnt sienna and use the no. 12 brush to add lighter lines connected with the darker foliage lines. Do the same with another mix of Naples yellow and sap green.

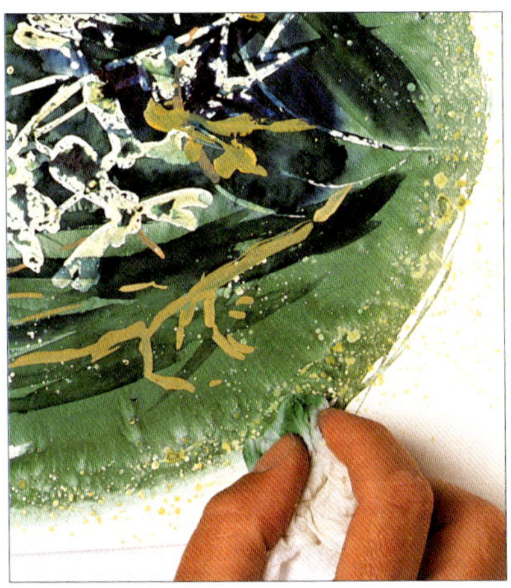

7. Remove paint from the surface of the masking fluid using kitchen paper and clean water, so that it will not rub into the paper. Then rub off the masking fluid with dry, clean kitchen paper.

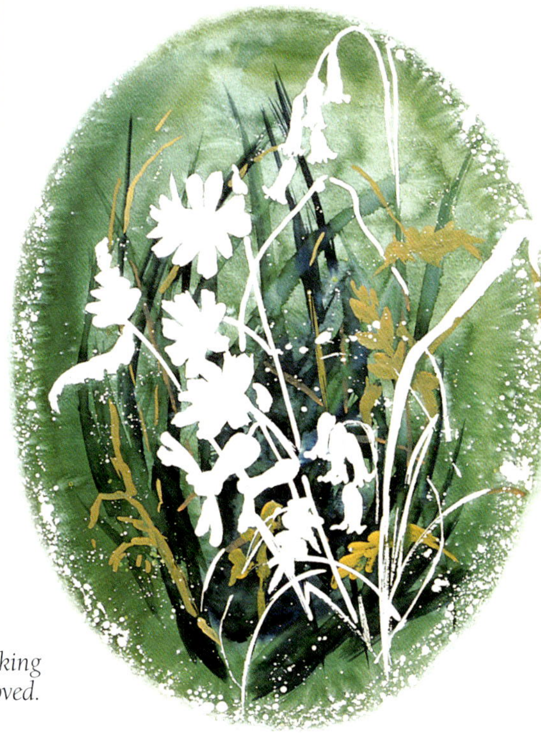

The painting with the masking fluid removed.

8. Make a very thin mix of ultramarine blue and magenta and paint the bluebells.

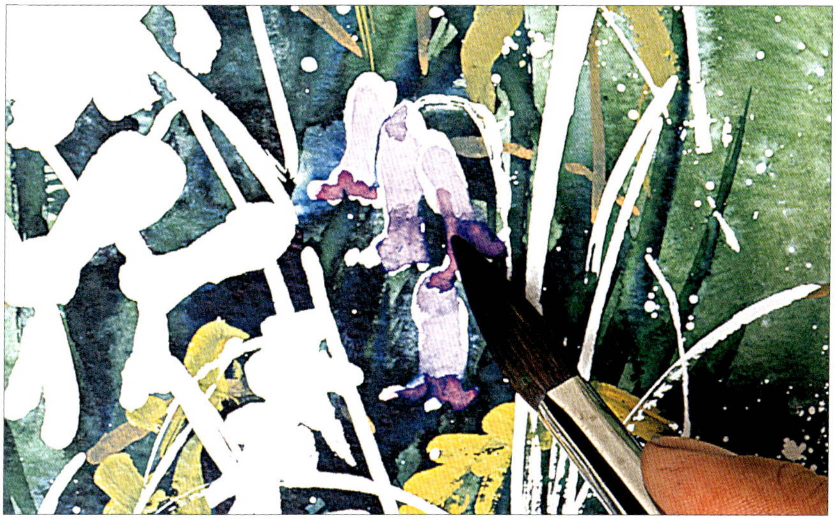

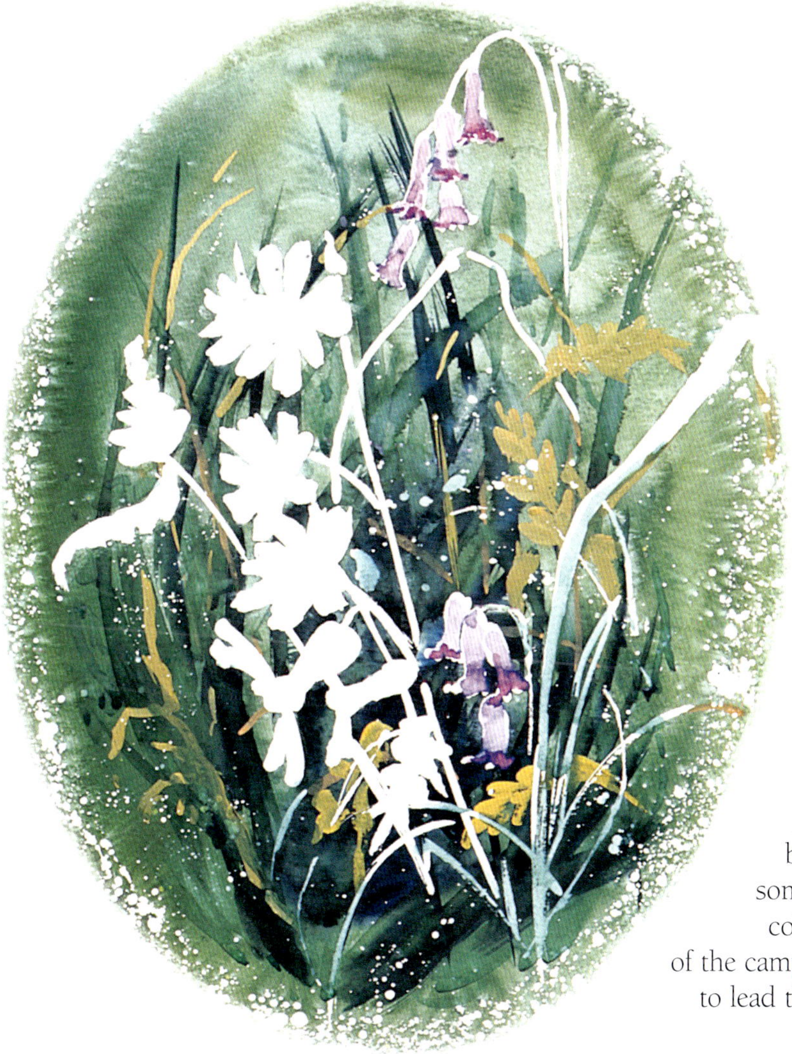

9. Use the no. 10 brush and dilute sap green and azure blue to add cool greens in the shaded area at the bottom of the composition. Add some distant grasses, too. The cool colour will emphasise the warmth of the campions later. Use the foliage lines to lead the eye round the image, linking various elements.

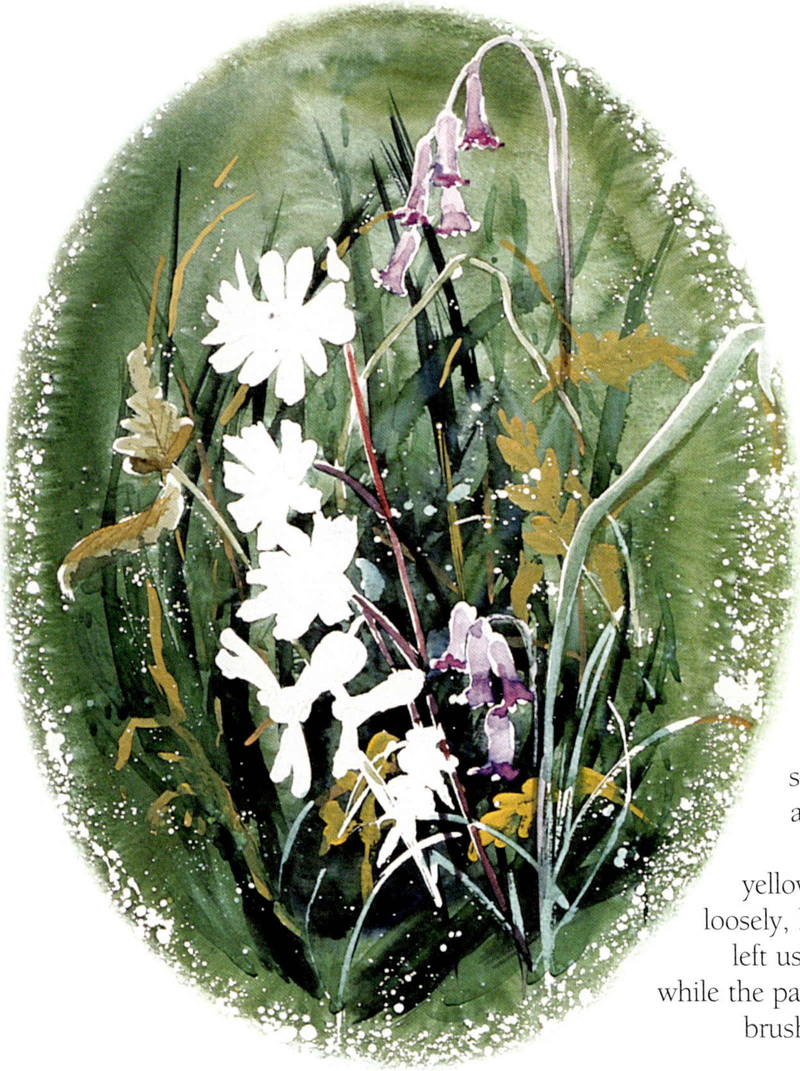

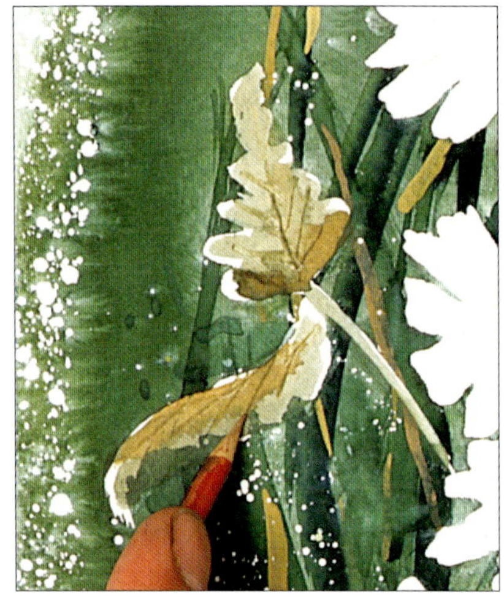

10. Mix magenta and burnt sienna darkened with a tiny touch of ultramarine blue for the stems. Leave some white edges to suggest that they are lit from one side. Darken towards the bottom of the stems with more blue. Mix ultramarine blue and a tiny bit of Naples yellow for the stalks of the bluebells, and sap green and Naples yellow for other stalks, which should be painted loosely, leaving some white. Paint oak leaves on the left using this same mix and add marigold yellow while the paint is wet. Use the sharpened end of an old brush to indent lines for the veins on the leaves.

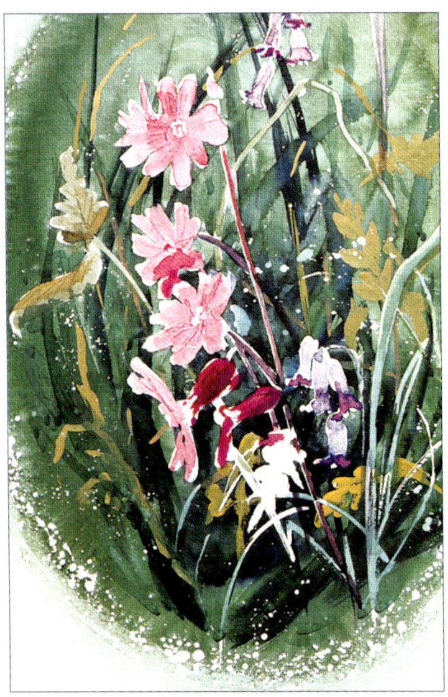

11. Now paint the campions using magenta and flame red, darkened in places with ultramarine blue. Indent to make the fine lines in the flowers. Add pale touches to the flower centres and define the lit sides of the stalks using permanent white. Mix white with the petal colour to lighten one or two of the petals.

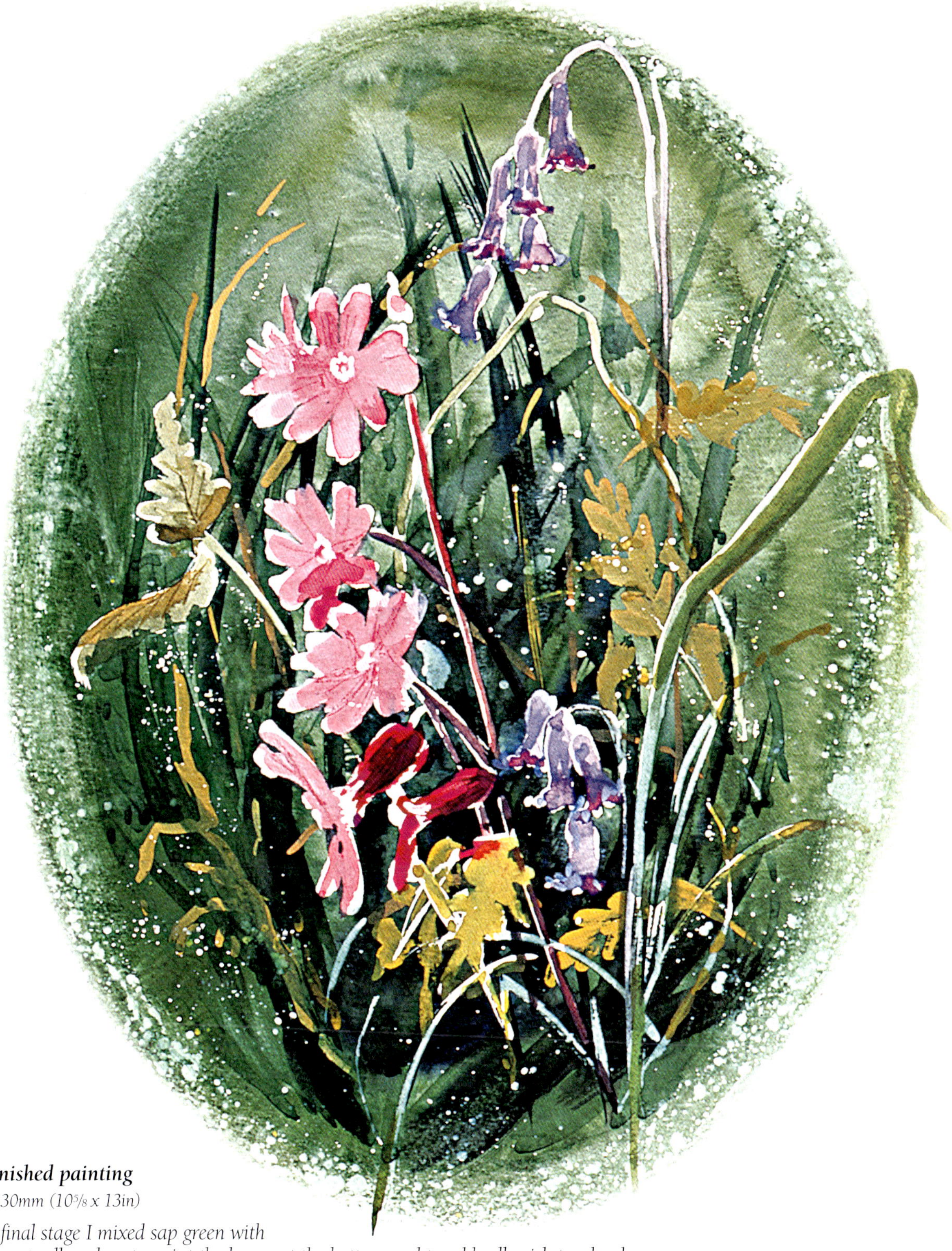

The finished painting

270 x 330mm (10⁵⁄₈ x 13in)

At the final stage I mixed sap green with permanent yellow deep to paint the leaves at the bottom and to add yellowish touches here and there. I softened the edges by rubbing them with damp kitchen paper, and painted a blade of grass going out of the oval. Finally I added more blue to the bluebells using a mix of dilute azure blue, ultramarine blue and white.

Flower Study

210 x 300mm (8¼ x 11¾in)

This was painted as a demonstration at a nearby horticultural college, where I tutored a painting group. You can see the spattering technique around the edge, the masking technique in the blooms, and the lifting out technique in the leaves. The flowers in the background were painted wet in wet, so that the slightly blurred edges would make them appear to recede.

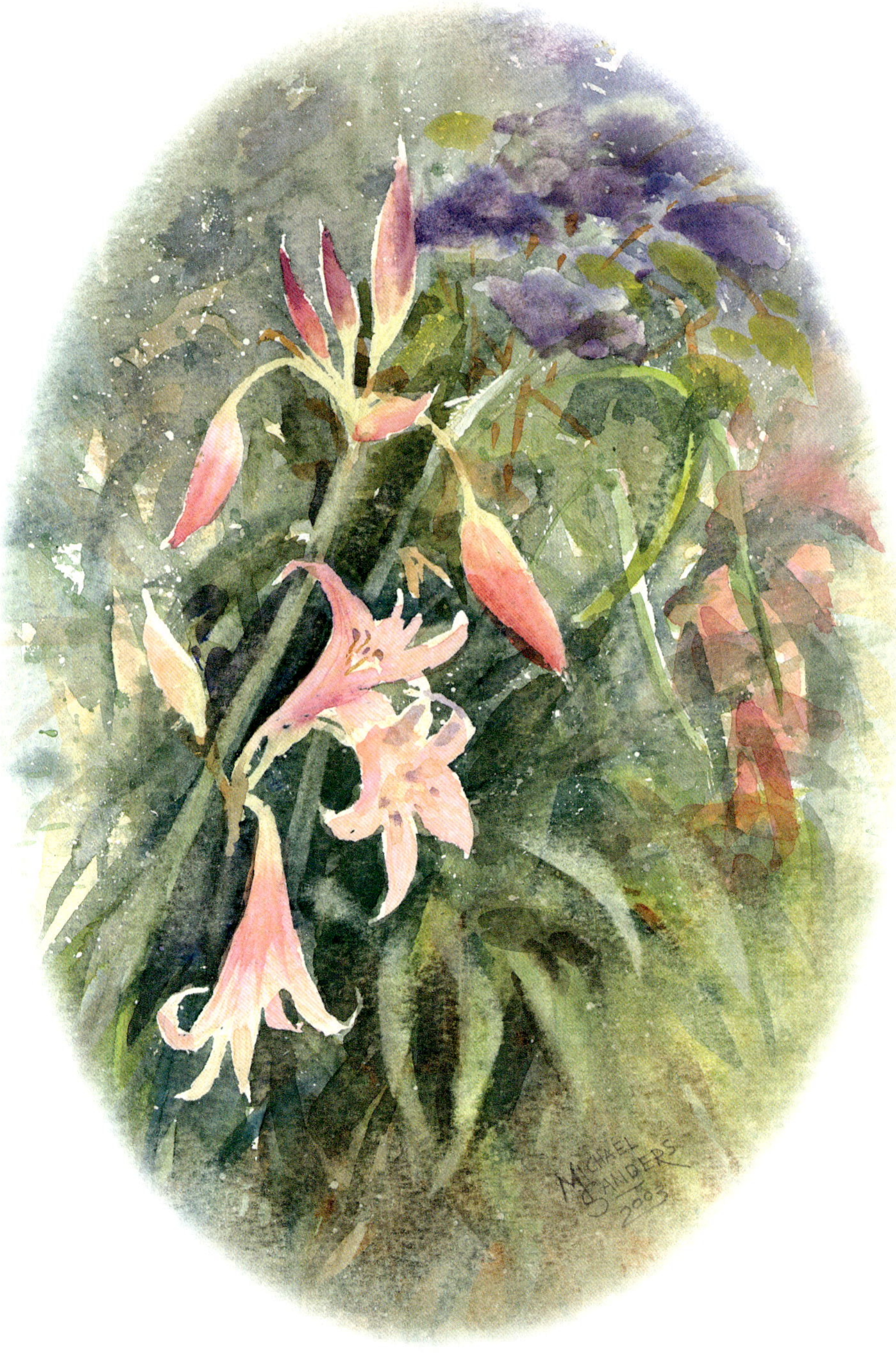

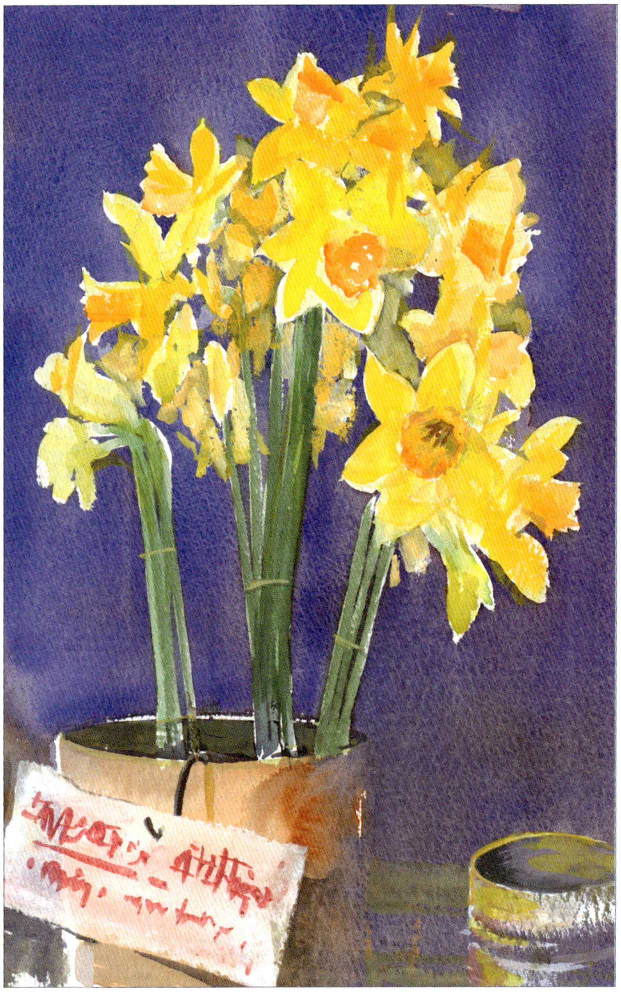

Daffodils for Sale

210 x 340mm (8$\frac{1}{4}$ x 13$\frac{3}{8}$in)

This is a nice example of masking a mass of blooms, rather than individuals. The stalks were masked and the light rim at the top of the jar. I chose a simple violet blue background because of the orange and yellow colour of the subject. Note that only two or three of the flowers are painted in detail, the rest are simply an impression.

Flower Detail

190 x 290mm (7$\frac{1}{2}$ x 11$\frac{1}{2}$in)

This little image includes the use of indenting into the leaves to show the veins. A cocktail stick was used for this while the paint was still wet, and then a touch of burnt sienna was dropped on to the leaf edges. This was all done before the masking fluid on the blooms had been removed. Alizarin crimson and magenta were applied to the flowers, wet in wet, and allowed to run and merge.

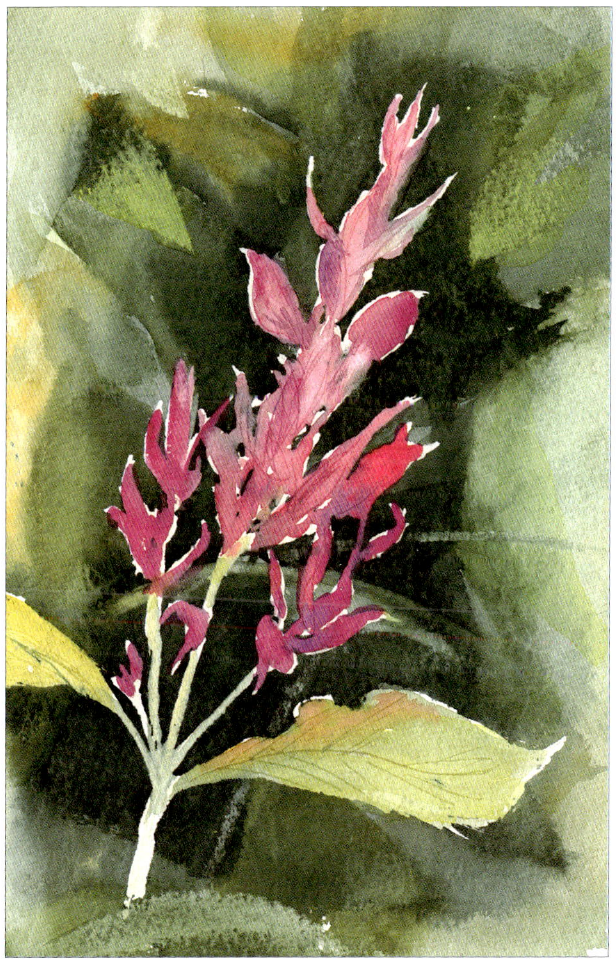

Mediterranean River

Here I have taken my source photograph, of Bosa in Sardinia, and selected a section of it to make into a painting. If you look closely at the photograph, you will see a grid drawn on it. This helps to transfer the image on to a larger surface ready for painting. By drawing a simple grid on the board, either with a soft pencil or dilute paint, you will be able to concentrate on just one rectangle at a time, rather than a mass of confusing detail.

You will need

- Burgundy coloured board, 295 x 420mm (11⅝ x 16½in)
- A scrap of watercolour paper
- Colours: permanent white, azure blue, ultramarine blue, magenta, Naples yellow, marigold yellow, burnt sienna, flame red, permanent yellow deep, turquoise blue and lemon yellow
- 2.5cm (1in) hake brush, no. 10 and no. 12 round brushes

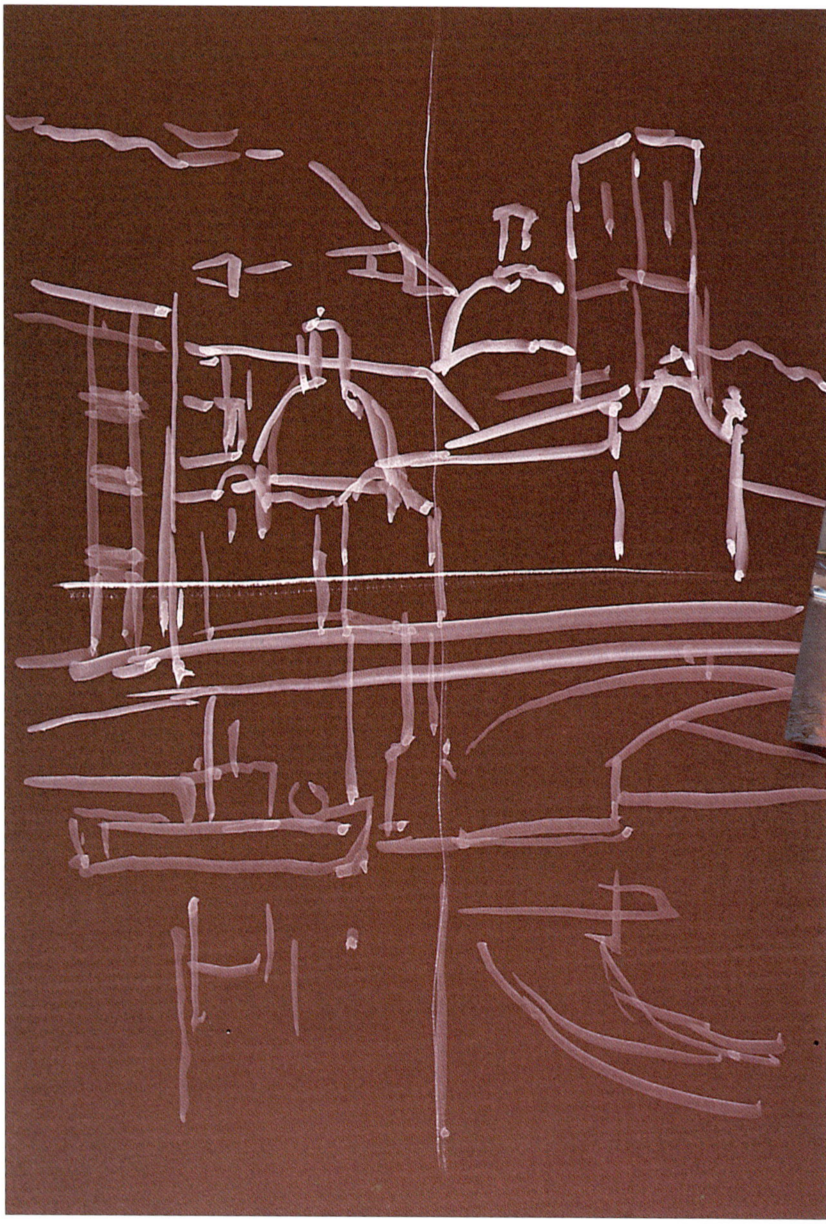

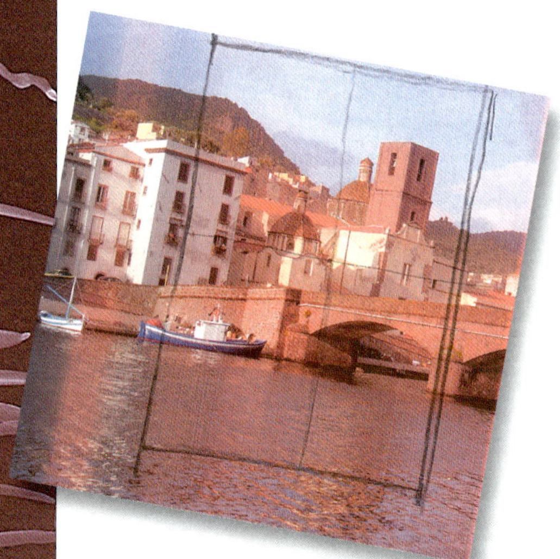

1. Transfer the image from the grid using dilute white paint and the no. 12 brush.

2. Mix a sky blue from azure blue, ultramarine blue and permanent white. Dilute it until it flows well and block in the sky using the hake brush. Brush in some sky reflections in the river.

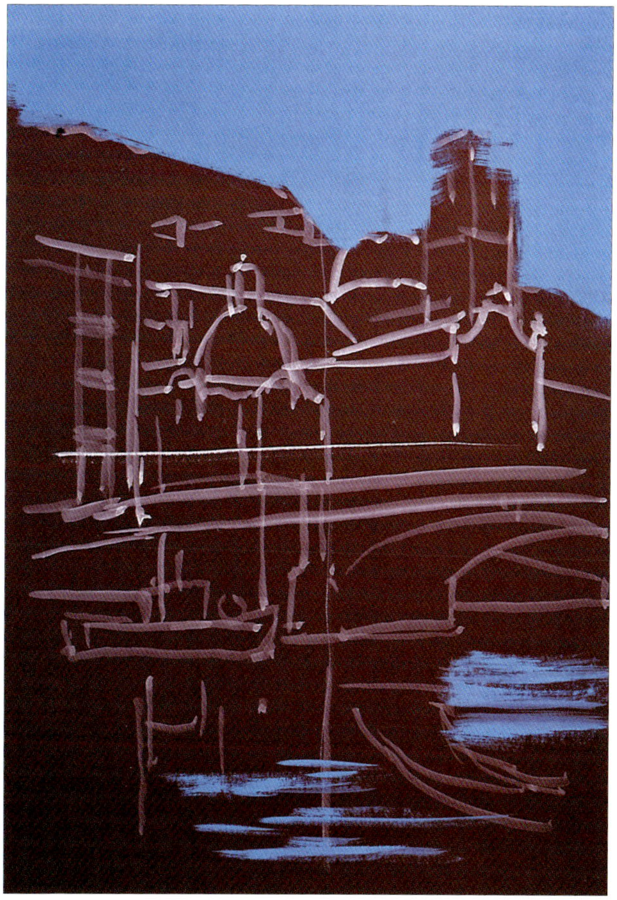

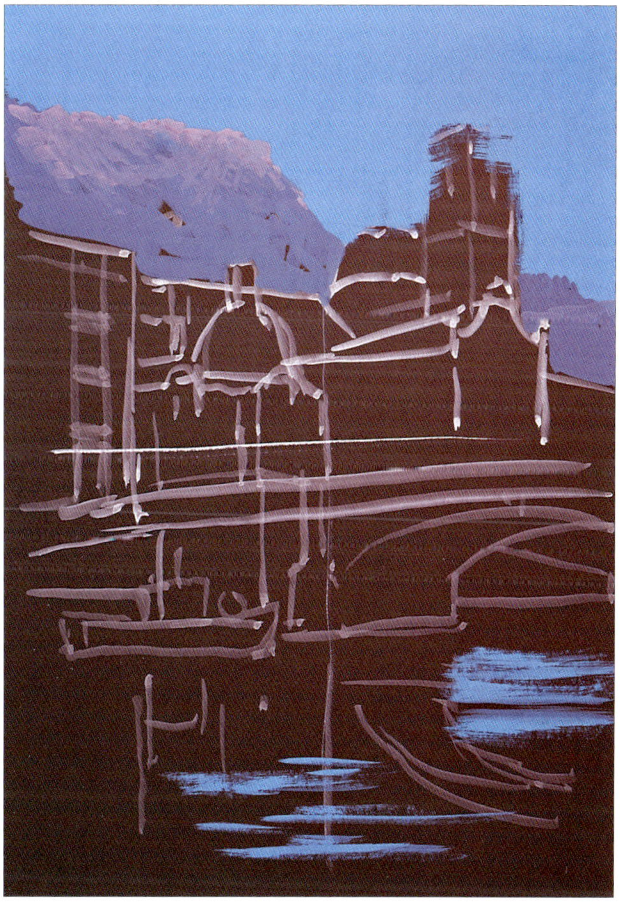

3. Mix the sky blue with magenta and Naples yellow and block in the distant headland in purply grey, using the no. 10 brush. Your brush strokes should follow the shape of the land. Paint over the edges of the distant buildings, since these will be painted in later using the opaque technique. Mix magenta and white to make a paler colour for the top of the distant hill.

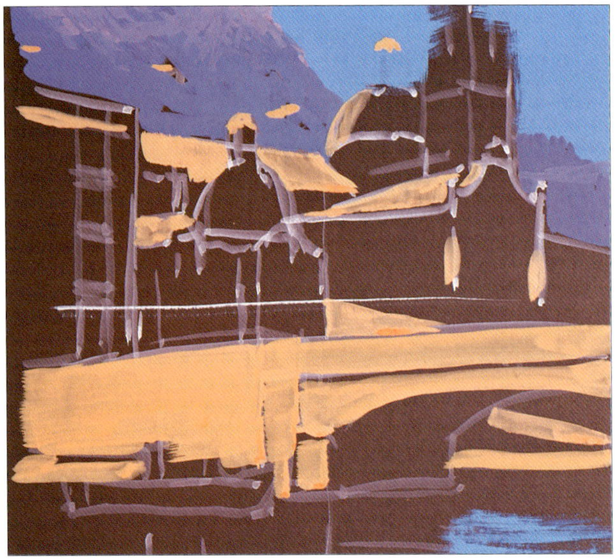

4. Use a mix of magenta, Naples yellow and marigold yellow to block in the shapes of the roofs and the top of the dome. Add a touch of burnt sienna and block in the bridge, painting over where the boat will be, since you will use an opaque technique to paint this in later.

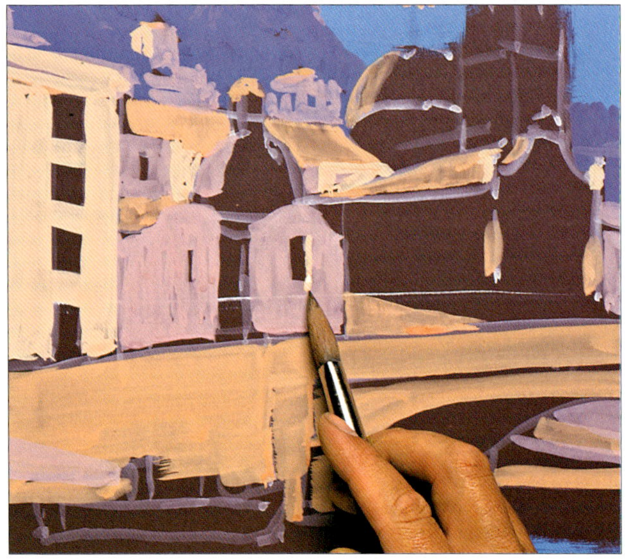

5. Use the no. 10 brush and magenta, Naples yellow and the sky blue for the shadow area of some buildings. Keep the mix fairly thin so that some of the background colour will show through when it is dry. Suggest some architectural details by leaving the background showing. Use the same mix to suggest houses on the distant hill. Lighten it with Naples yellow for the building on the left-hand side, leaving the background colour for the windows.

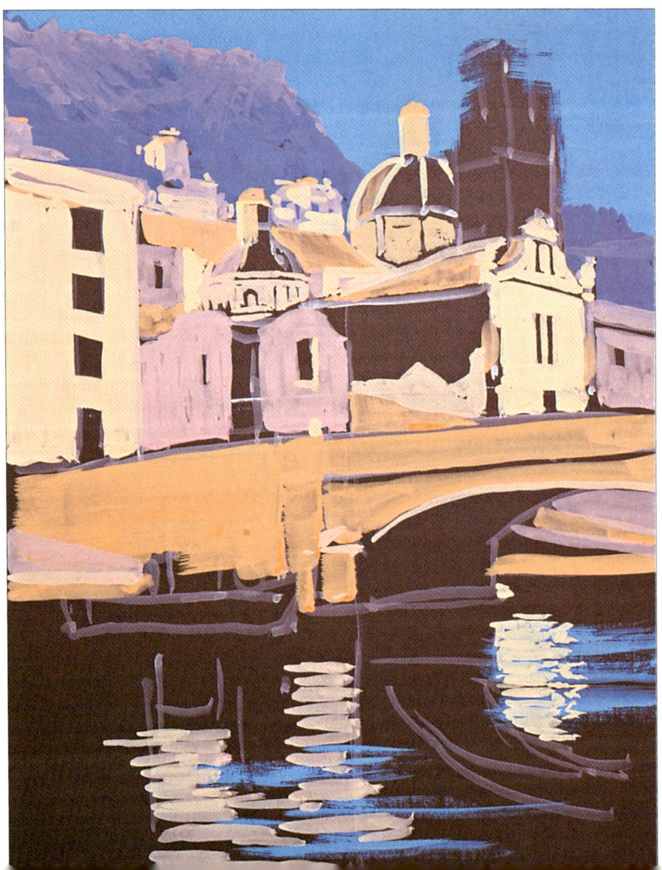

6. Mix Naples yellow and white with a hint of burnt sienna and paint in the lighter areas of the buildings, leaving gaps to suggest architectural details. Start to add reflections in the river with horizontal strokes of the no. 10 brush.

7. Add red to the roofs using flame red and Naples yellow and painting over previous colours. Paint in tiles, window frames and other details. Add a little magenta for shadowed areas and burnt sienna and a hint of the sky blue for the two domes. Paint the domes in segments, leaving the underpainting showing through. Lighten the more distant one with a touch of white to make it appear to recede. Add white to paint the big tower, then add a touch of Naples yellow for the lighter side, and a little sky blue for the shadowed side. Put in a touch more blue and paint the dark stonework areas on top of the tower, and the dark edge of the small dome. Use the same colours to paint the reflection of the tower in horizontal strokes.

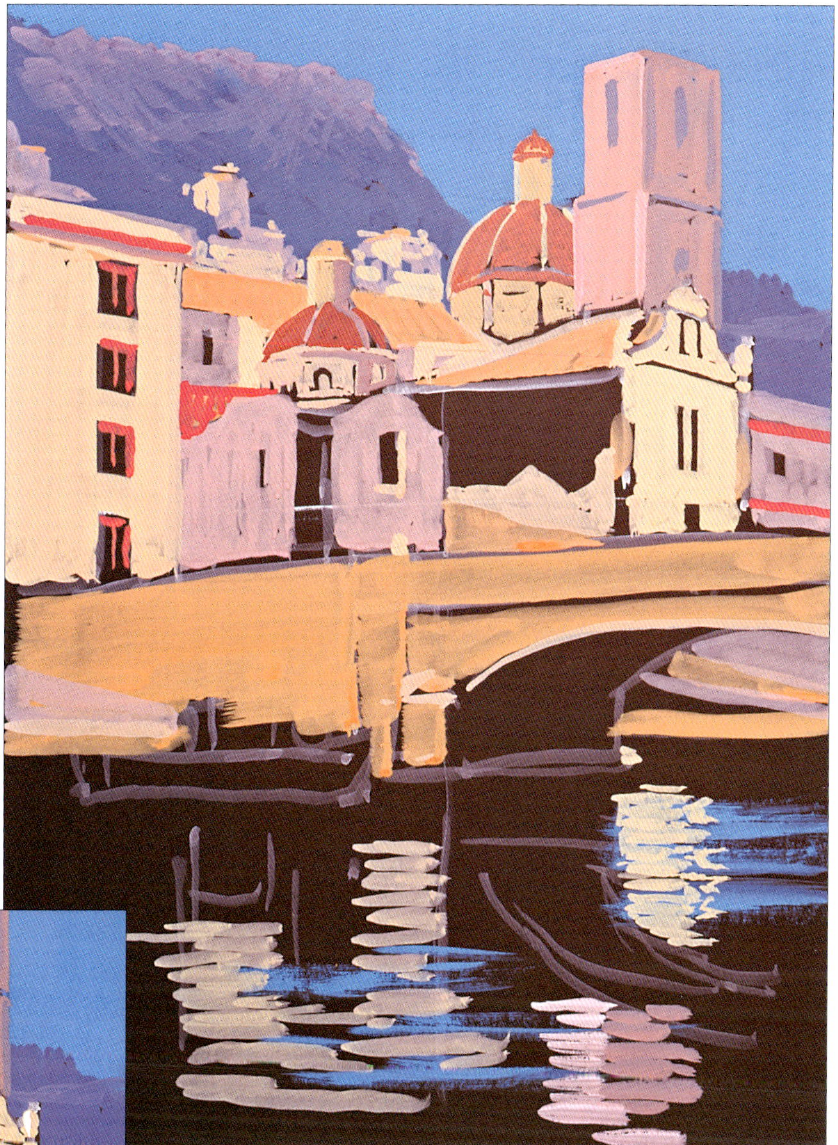

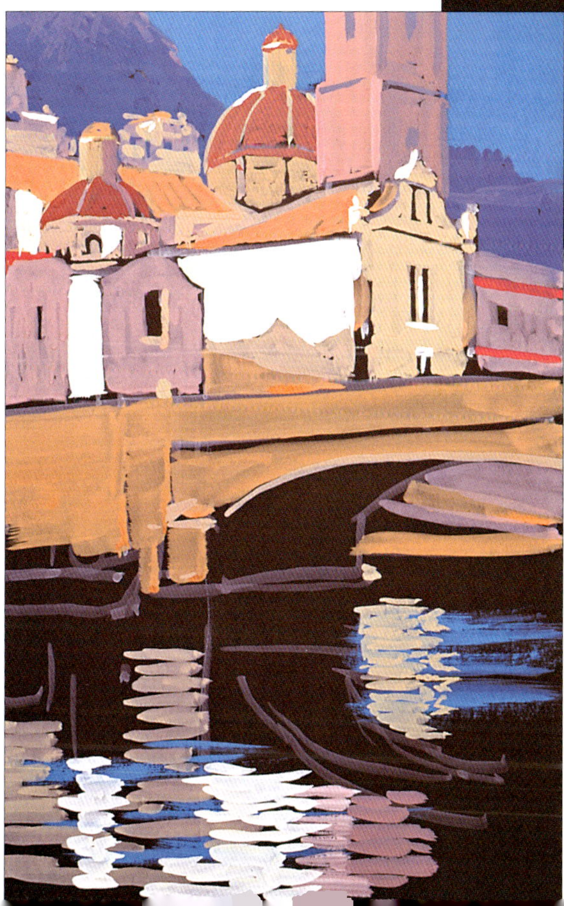

8. Make a thick mix of permanent white and permanent yellow deep for the highlights of the buildings. Add the same colour to the reflections.

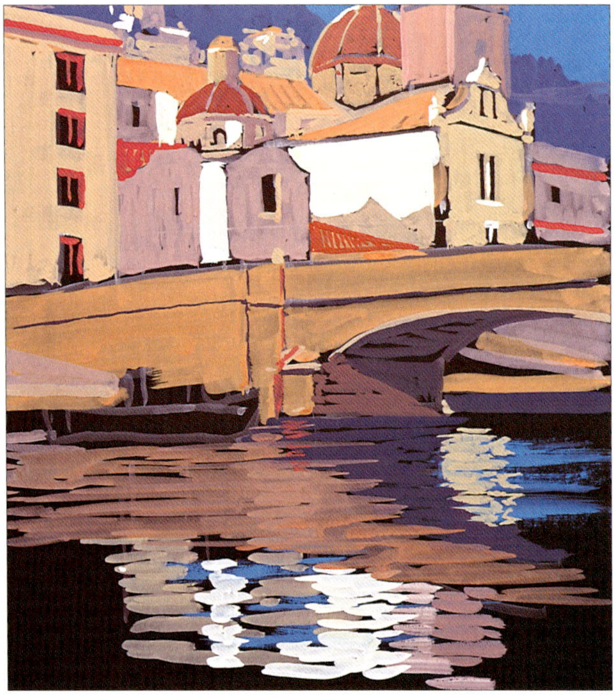

9. Paint under the arch of the bridge with a darkish purple mixed from ultramarine blue, magenta, burnt sienna and a touch of white. Paint the dark line along the bridge. Add flame red and white to lighten where the underside of the bridge catches the light. Add more ultramarine blue and magenta for the water under the bridge and the bank seen through the arch. Darken the colours used for the buildings with burnt sienna to paint the left-hand side of the water where the boat will go. Add the bridge colour to the water in broad, horizontal strokes. Then add a touch of magenta to the bridge and to its reflection.

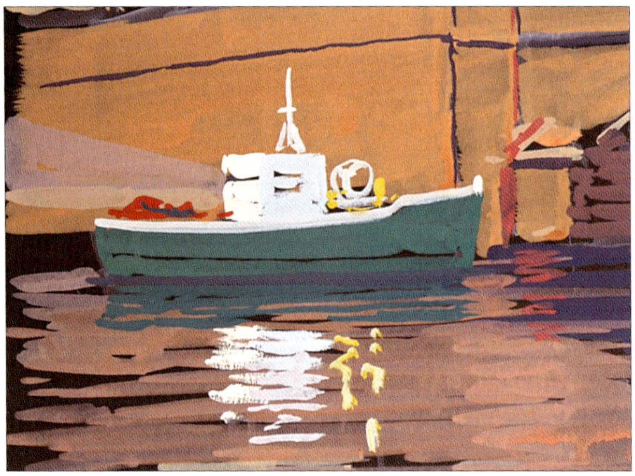

10. Paint the hull of the boat in a bright blue-green mixed from turquoise blue, lemon yellow and white. Paint the cabin and its reflection in permanent white and Naples yellow. Darken the hull colour with a touch of azure blue and burnt sienna, and add the reflection directly underneath. Use the same colour to add definition to the top of the boat. Add bright yellow for details and their reflections, and red made from flame red and burnt sienna. Paint the base of the boat at the waterline with a darker blue-green made from the hull colour with a touch of ultramarine.

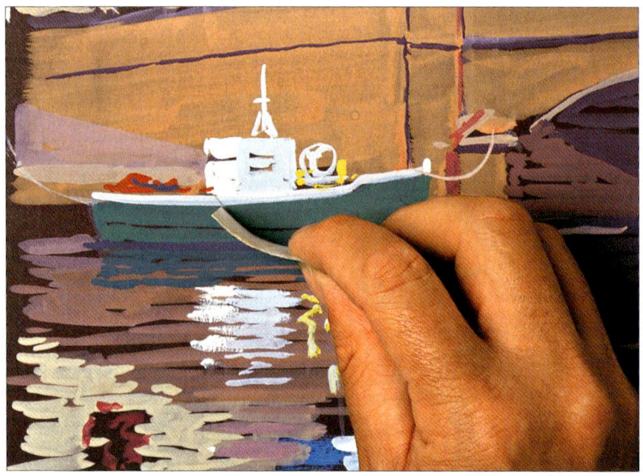

11. With horizontal strokes of the brush, paint the reflection of the building on the left, leaving gaps for the window darks. To paint the ropes mooring the boat, dampen a bit of watercolour paper and use the edge to scrape up the white paint mix. Curve the paper and apply the paint as shown.

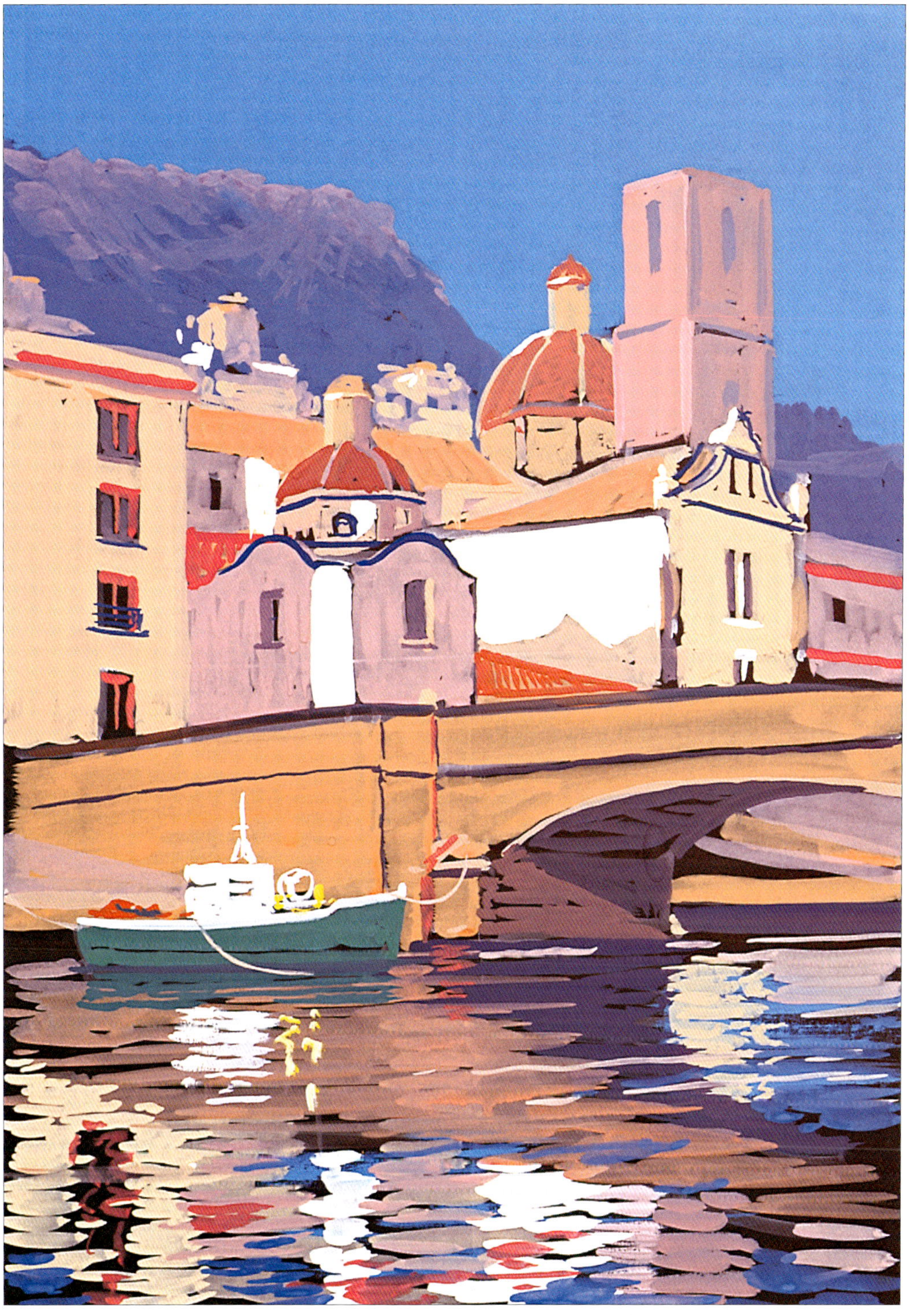

The finished painting

280 x 405mm (11 x 16in)

This painting expresses the heat and vibrancy of the experience of being there, rather than absolute realism. If you wish, you can add some additional little touches of pale Naples yellow or pale burnt sienna here and there, to break up any colours that look too even – but don't overdo it!

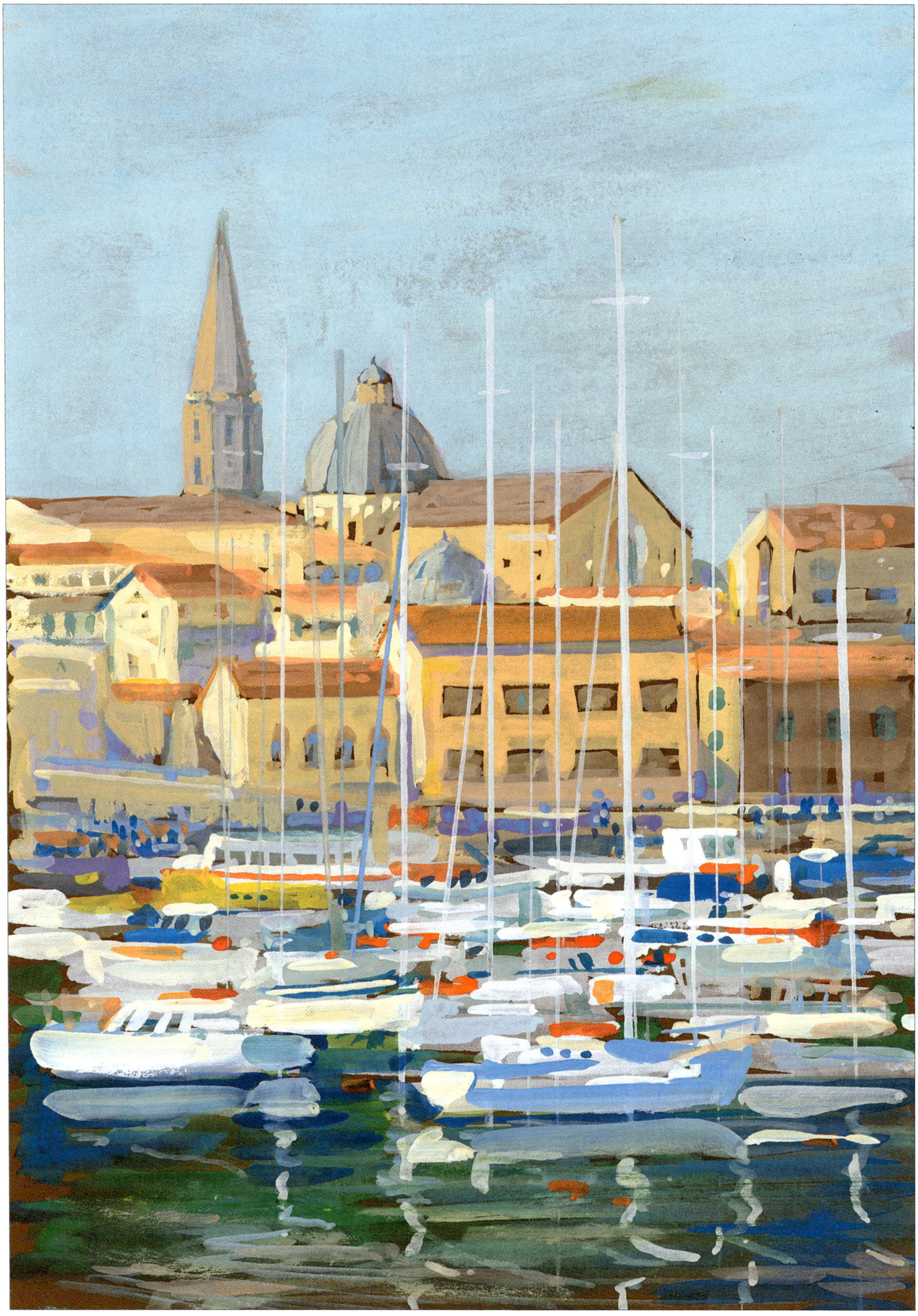

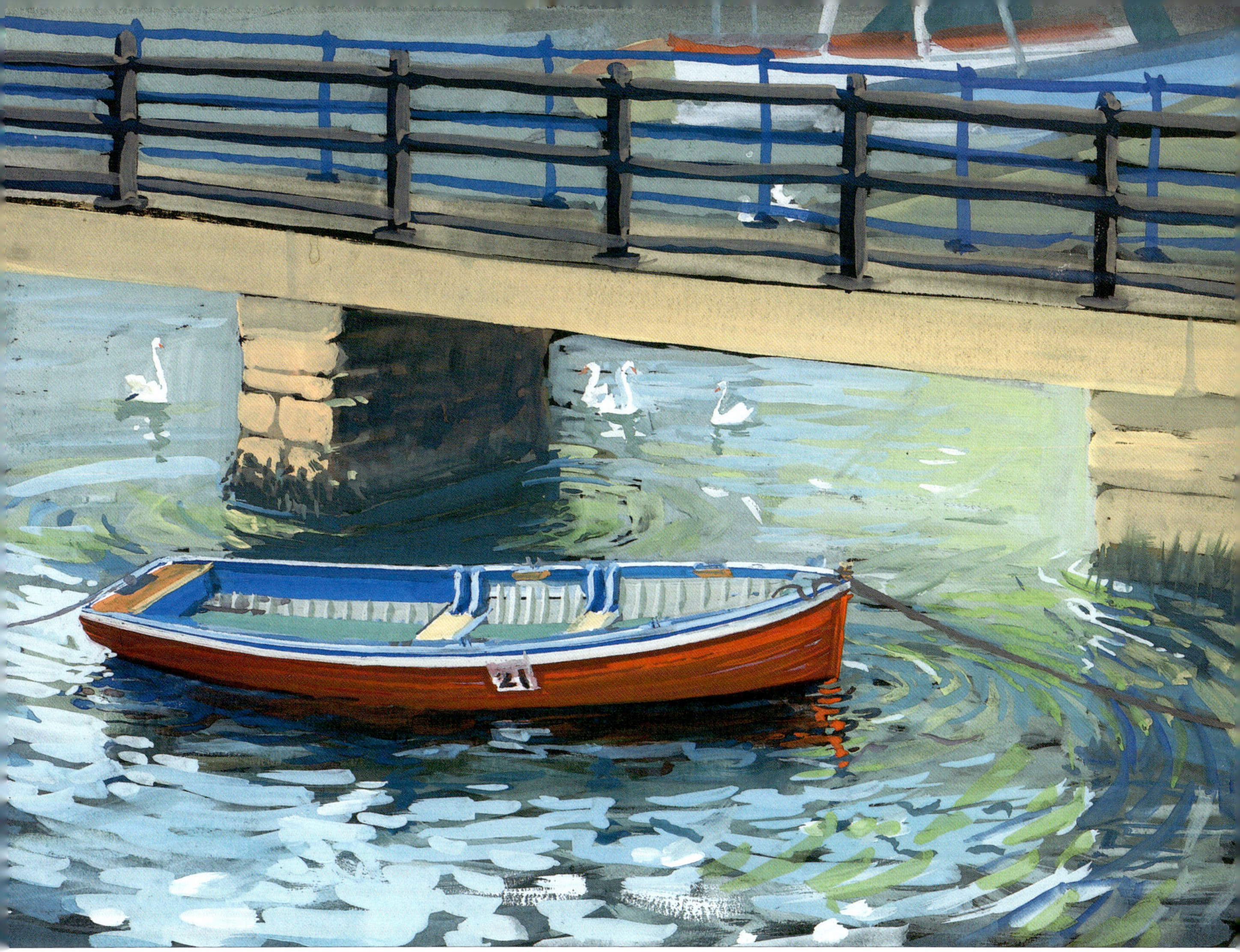

The Red Boat

250 x 175mm (9¾ x 7in)

This is a view from the window of one of the venues in Cornwall where I run classes. It looks down into the River Tamar, and the scene is always changing. There had been a discussion about gouache and what it could do, so I did this little painting on a scrap of black card, using a 1.25cm (½in) flat brush, as a class demonstration. There were so many questions about it afterwards; that's when I decided a book was necessary!

Opposite

Alghero Harbour, Sardinia

180 x 265mm (7⅛ x 10½in)

This was a challenge! A busy mass of masts, boats and vibrant colours, with everything seeming to move and shimmer in the heat. I tried this scene three times; this is the third attempt. The first two were very detailed and I quickly got lost in complicated shapes and distractions. I was sitting near a car park beside a busy road, and had no shortage of interested bystanders. In the end, I decided to paint the effect, rather than the detail, and this is the result. I must say, it turned out better than I thought it would.

Index

aerial perspective 24
architectural details 42

background 32, 39, 48
board 11
 coloured 40
brushes 12, 20
 cleaning 24
 flat 47
 hake 10, 22, 23, 26, 32, 33, 40, 41
 household 10, 21, 22, 28
 no. 6 round 22, 27
 no. 10 round 32, 35, 40, 41, 42, 44
 no. 12 round 22, 26, 32, 34, 40
 watercolour 10

card 21, 33
 coloured 4, 7, 9, 22, 47
colour
 background 8, 9, 24, 42
 complementary 17
 receding 17, 43
 temperature 7, 14, 17
 wheel 12
connecting 16, 18, 36

distance 14, 17, 18, 20

foreground 17, 18, 21, 23, 25, 27, 30, 48

highlights 14, 28, 43

indenting 21, 36, 39

lifting out 21, 38

masking fluid 11, 20, 32, 33, 34, 39
masking tape 11, 32
masking technique 20, 38, 39

negative shapes 21, 27

opacity 4, 6, 9, 20
opaque technique 8, 41
outdoors 4, 10

palette 11, 12
paper 20
 coloured 7, 9, 48
 watercolour 8, 12, 20, 32, 33, 40
 wetting 20, 30
photographs 17, 40

reflections 41, 43, 44

scraping up 30, 44
sgraffito 21, 29
shadows 14, 26, 42, 43
simplification 18
spattering 21, 28, 29, 30, 38
sponging 4, 11, 21, 29, 30

texture 4, 16, 21, 25
thumbnail sketches 16, 18, 32
tone 13, 14, 16

wet in wet 20, 29, 38, 39, 48
wet on dry 20, 29, 48

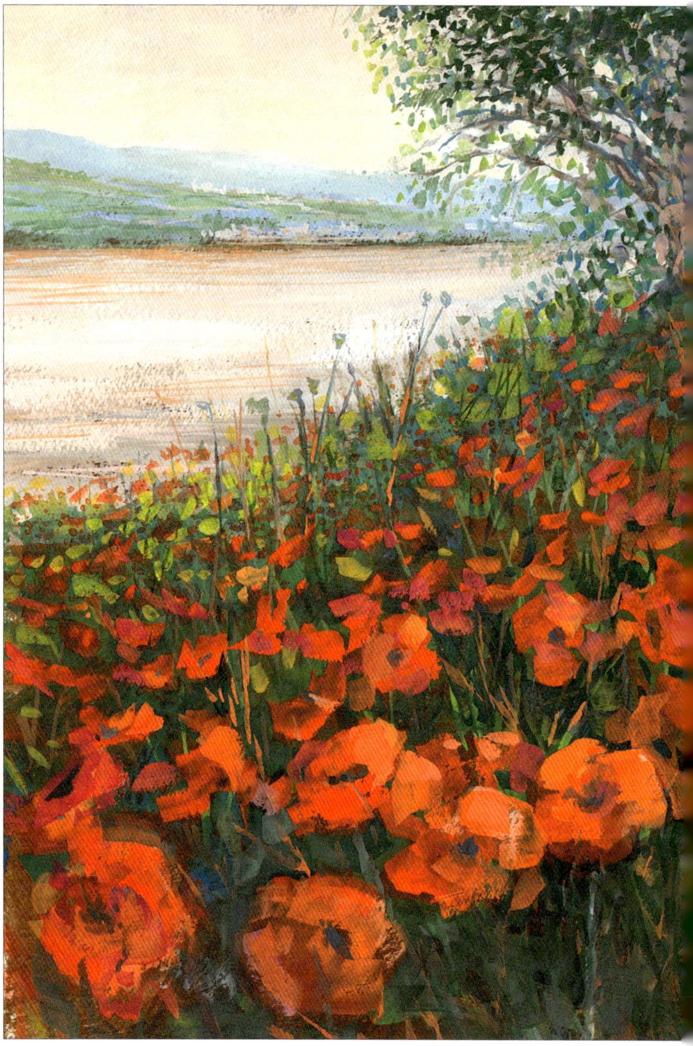

Estuary Poppies

240 x 325mm (9½ x 12¾in)

I paint poppies a lot; for me they evoke a sense of time and place. These were painted on brown paper, with quite a bit of the background showing through. The distant ones were painted wet in wet, on top of a mid-green. Foregrounds need to be harder edged, so they are done wet on dry. Little light touches of pale green near the water's edge stop the contrast being too great in that area, and impart a sunny feel. There is an accidental streak in the distance near the shoreline; it looked like a row of cottages, so I added the hint of a few chimneys and left it.